FAT HEAD KIDS

STUFF ABOUT DIET AND HEALTH
I WISH I KNEW
WHEN I WAS YOUR AGE

WRITTEN BY TOM NAUGHTON
ILLUSTRATED BY CHAREVA NAUGHTON

MIDDLE ROAD PICTURES

Published by Middle Road Pictures, Franklin TN, United States of America.

Special thanks to NASA and STScI for the use of the public domain image of the Carina Nebula Pillar available at www.HubbleSite.com.

Fat Head Kids: Stuff About Diet and Health I Wish I Knew When I Was Your Age / Tom Naughton

ISBN: 978-0-9986734-0-0

Designed by Chareva Naughton. The typeface used are Helvetica and Expo2.

For more information about Tom Naughton's other works, please visit www.FatHead-Movie.com.

Contents

INTRODUCTION

You probably remember someone like me from grade school. I was what the other kids called "a brain." But that was almost 50 years ago, and I'm told kids nowadays wouldn't insult me like that. Today they'd call me a *nerd*, a *dork*, or possibly a *dweeb*. Anyway, you know the type. I was usually the smartest kid in class, and I was lousy at sports.

How lousy? Well, here's one of my not-so-fond memories from gym class: We were running a relay race where each guy on the team had to dribble a basketball down the court, make a layup, then dribble back and hand off to the next guy. I was the last guy on our team, and when I got the ball, we were in the lead. I bounced the ball down the court, tossed it towards the basket ... and missed. By a lot. I tried again and missed. And missed again. And again — mostly because my weak arms couldn't fling the ball high enough.

The other team had already won, but the gym teacher growled, "You're not quitting until you make that basket." So I leaned back and hurled the ball as hard as I could. It bounced off the rim, smacked me in the face, and knocked me on my butt. At that point, the gym teacher decided I could quit after all.

Around age 13, something happened to my skinny body I didn't think was possible: I started getting fat. But I didn't become one of those big, strong, fat guys. Nope. I had skinny arms and legs, a fat belly and — most embarrassing of all — boy boobs.

I wasn't fast even when I was skinny, but getting fat gave me the speed of a turtle. When I was in seventh grade, yet another gym teacher had us run a relay race. Once again, I was the last man on our team, and we were leading when it was my turn to run. When the last guy on the other team saw he was racing me, he didn't bother running. Instead, he skipped to the finish line. Do you have any idea how embarrassing it is to lose a race to a guy who's skipping?

Meanwhile, I was running as fast as I could ... and my boy-boobs were slapping me so hard, it was like running with the Three Stooges. That's when I came to appreciate the kindness and compassion that's so common among adolescent boys.

And so, like millions of fat people before me, I came up with a plan:

I'll just starve myself until I'm as skinny as they are. Then they can't make fun of me for being fat.

I went on my first diet when I was 14. I counted every calorie and only ate 1500 of them per day. The results were unbelievable: I spent weeks feeling hungry, cranky and tired without shrinking my belly. And so, like millions of fat people before me, I gave up.

But, like millions of fat people before me, I kept trying. Over the decades, I went on all kinds of low-fat, low-calorie diets. But I didn't shrink my belly. Or I'd lose a little weight, then gain it back. As an adult, I spent countless hours jogging and walking on treadmills. But I didn't shrink my belly.

And every time I failed to lose weight, I knew exactly who to blame: me.

I realize now I didn't fail. The diets failed. The exercise programs failed. They failed because they're based on beliefs about weight loss that simply aren't true. I finally figured that out when I made a documentary called *Fat Head*.

I read a ton of research while making *Fat Head*, and when I put what I learned into action, I finally lost the weight and kept it off. And it wasn't just the extra fat that went away. I also waved goodbye to a bunch of annoying health problems.

So in my fifties, I finally had something like the body I wanted when I was in high school. Well, okay, when I was high school I wanted to look like this ...

... but this is pretty good, considering I spent most of my life as a fat guy.

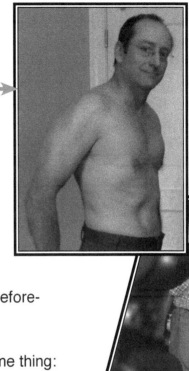

After *Fat Head* was released, hundreds of people sent me emails telling me how happy they were to finally lose weight. Sometimes they included before-and-after pictures.

Lots of people who emailed me said pretty much the same thing: I'm glad I finally lost weight and got healthy ... but man, I wish I'd known this stuff when I was a kid. My whole life could have been different.

Same goes for me. If I'd known then what I know now, my whole life could have been different too. So that's what you'll learn from this book: important stuff about diet and health I wish I knew when I was your age.

Ray

Rae

Phil

1

GETTING FAT ISN'T ABOUT CHARACTER

FAT HEAD KIDS
Stuff I Wish I Knew
When I Was Your Age

Since much of this book is about why kids get fat, I'm probably supposed to stop here and show some charts to prove that childhood obesity is a big problem. I'm not going to do that, and here's why: I went to school in the 1960s, and yes, things were different then. We had maybe one or two fat kids in each class.

And you know what? After I became one of them, I never once got together with the other fat kid in class and said:

It's no fun being a fat kid, period. If you've been getting fat, I know you want to change that. And I'll bet at least a few people have already told you why you're fat and what to do about it — like the classmates who explained it to me.

ISN'T IT GREAT THAT WE'RE THE ONLY ONES?

YES, I'M SO HAPPY OUR CLASSMATES ARE ALL SKINNY ENOUGH TO MAKE FUN OF US.

NICE BOOBS, FAT BOY!

MAYBE YOU SHOULD SKIP A MEAL NOW AND THEN.

OR GET OFF YOUR BIG BUTT AND MOVE A LITTLE.

What these helpful young men were telling me is that people get fat because of a flaw in their character: They like to eat, so they eat too much, and then they get fat. So to lose weight, they just need to apply some willpower. Eat a little less, exercise a little more, or both.

Now ... let's suppose these guys grow up and become doctors, or dieticians, or personal trainers — and they learn it's not polite to make fun of fat people. They'll probably still give the same advice, especially if they've never been fat. Only now that advice will sound almost like science:

3

It's kind of strange if you think about it. Fifty years ago, very few Americans were overweight, but almost nobody counted calories. In fact, the calorie labels you see on food now didn't even exist until the 1990s.

Nowadays we have lots of fat people, and everyone seems to be talking about calories. ***Cut the calories, cut the calories, cut the calories!*** So what's a calorie?

To understand calories, let's forget about food for a minute and talk about something you wouldn't eat unless you're a termite: wood.

If you had a nice piece of wood, you could chop it into pieces and build something useful, like a chair. Or you could store the wood for later. Or you could toss it in a fireplace and burn it to produce heat. How much heat? Well, there are different units for measuring heat, but the common ones are BTUs (British Thermal Units), joules, and ... calories. So technically, a calorie is a unit of heat.

But heat is also a form of energy, and in our world, energy makes things happen. Back in the Old West, people burned wood to boil water to make steam. The steam could turn an engine big enough to move an entire train. So we could say the energy to move a train came from the **calories** in wood.

It's the same with food. To determine the calories in food, scientists burn it in something called a **calorimeter** and measure the heat. No, they're not trying to figure out how many pizzas you should burn to keep your house warm. They're measuring how much energy the food would produce if you burned it all for fuel.

A calorie is a unit of heat.

The energy to move a train came from the calories in wood.

But you don't burn all your food for fuel. Some of what you eat is broken down into building materials for the rest of your body. Some of it is converted to fat and stored in your fat cells. That way your body can burn fat for fuel between meals. If you couldn't store calories in your fat cells, you'd have to spend most of your life eating.

Because your body can store calories as fat, a lot of so-called experts (like my helpful classmates) think your body works like a savings account. I call that **The Piggy Bank Theory**, and it looks like this:

Every time you eat, you deposit calories in your body. Some of the food goes into your body's Building & Repair Fund, and some goes to pay your daily energy bill — the energy your body burns just to stay alive. But if there's any extra food left over, those

calories are automatically converted to fat and stored in your fat cells — like saving money in the Piggy Bank.

With a real piggy bank, it's easy to control how much you save. If you deposit $50 every week and withdraw $40, your piggy bank will grow by exactly $10 each week. If you deposit $50 every week and withdraw $60, your piggy bank will shrink by exactly $10 each week. It's a simple matter of calculating ***dollars in vs. dollars out.***

According to The Piggy Bank Theory, losing weight works by the same simple math. To shrink your fat cells, you just deposit fewer calories by eating less. Or you spend more on the energy bill by exercising. If you do either one, your body has to withdraw calories from the piggy bank, so you lose weight. It's a simple matter of calculating **calories in vs. calories out**.

People who believe in The Piggy Bank Theory will do things like drive to a gym, take an elevator to the workout room, then spend an hour on a treadmill walking nowhere. Or they write articles offering simple advice like this:

THIN AND HEALTHY? NAW, I'D RATHER HAVE THE BUTTER.

If you cut just one pat of butter from your daily diet and walk for just 20 minutes every day, you'll lose 20 pounds of fat in a year!

Well, that sounds easy, doesn't it?

So according to these people, if you're fat, it's because you're not willing to eat just a little less — which means you're a pig. Or you're not willing to exercise just a little more — which means you're a lazy pig.

But does that really make sense? Most fat people hate being fat. They spend billions of dollars on gym memberships, weight-loss clubs and weight-loss drugs. Are we supposed to believe they'd rather be fat than give up one pat of butter per day?

If people get fat because of their character, why are there more overweight babies now than 30 years ago? Did babies in previous generations drink less mother's milk so they wouldn't get fat? Did they go to baby-aerobics classes?

THAT'S ENOUGH, MOM! I'M ON A DIET!

FEEL THE BURP- ER, BURN!

If your body works like a bank account, how do we explain naturally thin people, like my wife? They have no idea how many calories they consume and eat whatever they like, but never gain weight. That's like making lots of deposits and withdrawals at your bank, without ever bothering to add them up ... and yet every time you check your balance, it's exactly 2,000 dollars.

Here's something else The Piggy Bank Theory can't explain:
We have two big dogs named Misha and Coco. They're sisters,
and we feed them exactly the same meals. Coco is bouncier
and more active than Misha, so she ought to burn more calories,
right? But Coco is 18 pounds heavier. In human terms, if Misha
weighed 180 pounds, Coco would weigh 212 pounds. When
we bought them as puppies, the breeder told us Coco would be
bigger. She never mentioned calories.

Obviously, there's something wrong with The Piggy Bank Theory.
Plenty of doctors and researchers have known that for years.

In a study from the 1960s, researchers wrote about obese patients who were locked in a hospital and fed just 600 calories each day. That's about one-fourth as much as most adults eat. And yet the obese patients didn't lose weight. Is that because of a flaw in their character? Should they only eat 300 calories per day? Or 200?

In an experiment at the Mayo Clinic, researchers had a group of volunteers eat an extra 1,000 calories every day for 56 days. According to The Piggy Bank Theory, those 56,000 extra calories should have made everyone 16 pounds fatter. But some people gained 10 times more body fat than others. The naturally-thin people barely gained any weight at all.

In another experiment, researchers took a group of mice and reduced their daily calories by five percent. That's the mouse version of **cut just one pat of butter per day from your diet**. They also used special lab equipment to make sure the mice were just as active as before.

5% MOUSE CHOW = 1 PAT BUTTER

Let's apply The Piggy Bank Theory and predict what happened:

1. They were eating less, so they made smaller deposits.
2. They were just as active, so their daily energy bill should have stayed the same.
3. Therefore, according to The Piggy Bank Theory, the mice had to withdraw calories from their fat cells to pay part of the energy bill. So their fat cells had to shrink.

But that's not what happened. When the mice were given less food, their fat cells got **bigger**, not smaller.

No wonder one scientist wrote this in an article about obesity:

The commonly held belief that obese individuals can ameliorate [improve] their condition by simply deciding to eat less and exercise more is at odds with compelling scientific evidence.

If your goal is to lose weight, let me ask you a question: Would your school hire a football coach who lost 97 percent of his games? Would your parents hire a piano teacher if 97 percent of her students never played any better ... and some ended up playing worse?

Of course not. But year after year, millions of people try to lose weight by following The Piggy Bank Theory. And year after year, 97 percent of them fail. In fact, many end up fatter than before.

People who believe in The Piggy Bank Theory argue that it's based on the Laws of Physics. Matter and energy can't just disappear or be created out of nothing. So to get bigger, you have to consume more calories than you burn.

That statement is true. But for explaining why people get fat, it's also meaningless. It's like saying Donald Trump is rich because he deposited more dollars in the bank than he spent. It's like saying if your toilet overflows, it's because more water went into the bowl than went out.

Yes, of course more water went into the bowl than went out. But that only explains **HOW** the toilet overflowed. It doesn't tell us **WHY** the toilet overflowed. The **WHY** in this case would be a clog in the drain pipe.

To fix a problem, you can't just describe **HOW** it happens. You also have to understand **WHY** it happens. We'll begin looking at **WHY** we get fat in the next chapter.

2

GETTING FAT IS ABOUT CHEMISTRY

As fans of The Piggy Bank Theory like to remind us, there are 3500 calories in a pound of fat. So **HOW** we get fat can be explained by simple math that looks like this

calories in – calories out = change in weight

But **WHY** we get fat isn't about math. It's about chemistry, which looks like this:

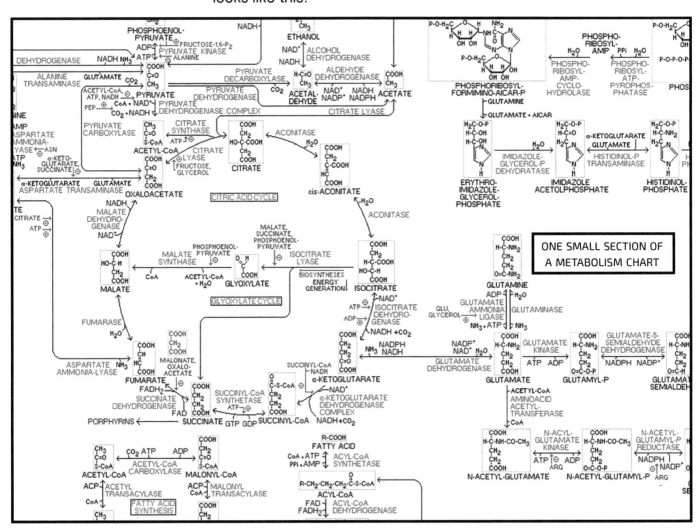

ONE SMALL SECTION OF A METABOLISM CHART

Don't worry; you don't need to understand all that chemistry. In fact, very few people understand all of it. What you need to understand is this:

Even when you're just sitting, your body is incredibly busy. Your lungs are breathing air. You heart is pumping blood. Your digestive system is breaking down food. Your muscles, organs and bones are generating millions of new cells. Your entire body is generating heat to keep you warm. And that's just a tiny fraction of what's going on inside of you right now.

Everything that happens in your body is triggered by chemical reactions, and those chemical reactions all use energy. Even the chemical reactions that convert food to energy burn energy. If we look at all the chemical reactions together (just a few are shown in the scary chart), they make up what scientists call your metabolism.

Your metabolism doesn't work like a piggy bank. Not even close. If anything, it's more like a super-complicated software application. So to understand how your body works, you need to understand how software works.

If you're like most kids these days, you already have some favorite software applications ... only you probably call them apps. My daughters love their apps, and I have to admit, some of them are pretty cool.

But even the coolest apps can **only do what they've been programmed to do** — not what you want them to do.

For example, when I'm playing Frisbee Golf on our Wii, I can't just decide I'm going to reach the green on the 17th hole with one throw. That's how I want the app to work, and in my opinion, that's how it should work. But an app doesn't know or care how we want it to work.

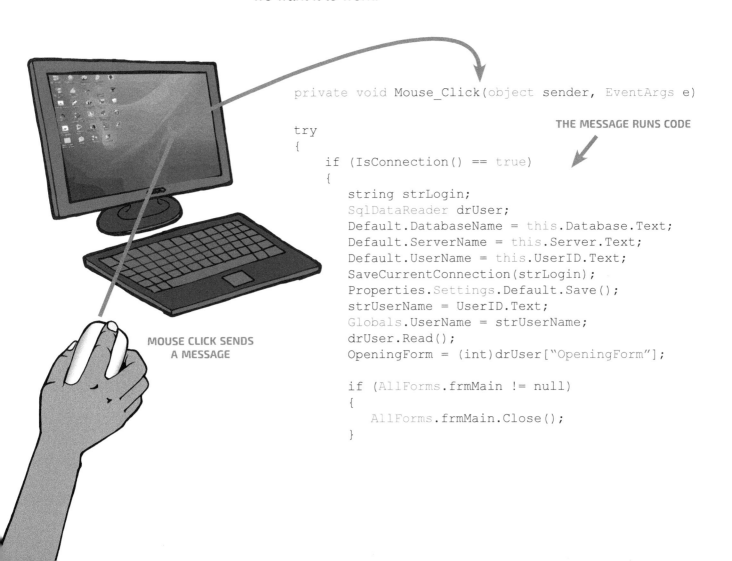

MOUSE CLICK SENDS
A MESSAGE

THE MESSAGE RUNS CODE

```
private void Mouse_Click(object sender, EventArgs e)

    try
    {
        if (IsConnection() == true)
        {
            string strLogin;
            SqlDataReader drUser;
            Default.DatabaseName = this.Database.Text;
            Default.ServerName = this.Server.Text;
            Default.UserName = this.UserID.Text;
            SaveCurrentConnection(strLogin);
            Properties.Settings.Default.Save();
            strUserName = UserID.Text;
            Globals.UserName = strUserName;
            drUser.Read();
            OpeningForm = (int)drUser["OpeningForm"];

            if (AllForms.frmMain != null)
            {
                AllForms.frmMain.Close();
            }
```

When you click a mouse, type on a keyboard, touch a screen, or work a remote, you send the app a message, otherwise known as a command. The app responds to the message by following the instructions that are written into its code — every single time. That's how all apps work.

To create apps for tablets and computers, software programmers (like me) write code in a language like C++ or Java. Your body is like a huge collection of biological apps. But these apps are programmed by Nature, and the code is written in chemistry. Everything about you — from the color of your eyes, to the sound of your voice, to the size of your belly — is the result of your body following instructions written into its chemical code.

So to understand **WHY** we get fat (and the other topics in this book), we need to forget about piggy banks and the stupidly simple math of *calories in vs. calories out*. Nothing in the human body is simple.

Instead, I want you to think of your body as a biological starship — one that's *waaaay* cooler than *The Enterprise*, *The Millennium Falcon* or any other starship you've seen in the movies. We'll call our starship The Nautilus.

Introducing ... **The Nautilus!**

The Nautilus is the amazing vehicle that carries you through the universe as you explore new worlds, save friendly creatures from the forces of evil, and occasionally get into trouble with your parents. You're in the captain's chair, so you can operate many of the ship's controls. You can decide where The Nautilus will go and what missions it will try to accomplish.

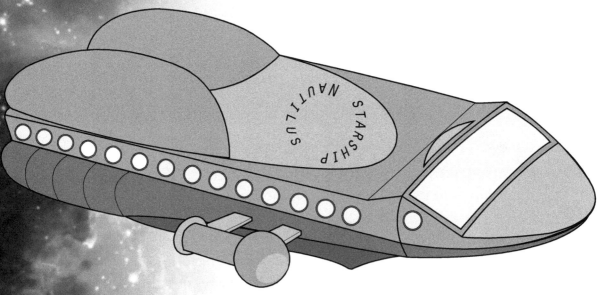

That's the good news. Now here's the not-so-good news: **you can't change how The Nautilus works**. It isn't like a modern aircraft that humans designed and can re-design when they need to. The Nautilus was designed and programmed by Nature at the dawn of time, and it's at least a thousand times more complicated than anything built by NASA. The best we can do is try to understand how it works.

Mr. Spot, the ship's science officer, has been studying The Nautilus for decades. So has Dr. Fishbones, the ship's medical officer. In spite of all their research, there's a lot they still don't know. But lucky for us, there's plenty they do know.

That's correct, captain. We know that The Nautilus depends on a super-computer we call The Brain. We know this super-computer is connected to the ship through a network called The Nervous System. We also know that the crew members are actually biological software applications — or what your Earth children call **apps**. They perform most of the ship's work automatically.

MR. SPOT
SCIENCE OFFFICER

Thanks for that dry, scientific explanation, Spot. Here's what you need to understand, Captain: life aboard The Nautilus is only possible because of how the crew members work together. Our crew is fantastic. Amazing. Stupendous. They're all that and a side of moonbeams, as your Earth children might say.

DR. FISHBONES
MEDICAL OFFICER

I'm pretty sure my Earth children wouldn't say that, but Dr. Fishbones is right about this: your body's biological apps are fantastic. No human programmer could create apps as brilliant as the ones that keep The Nautilus flying. But they're still apps — which means when they receive a message, *all they can do is follow the instructions written into their code*.

When you become a wizard with your favorite app, it means you've learned to send the right messages at the right time. It's the same with The Nautilus. The only way to improve your starship's performance is to change the messages you send to the crew. And guess what? **Everything you eat sends a chemical message**.

You have to eat, of course. As The Nautilus explores the universe, it burns a lot of fuel. It also requires daily rebuilding and repairs, which means it constantly needs new building materials. Fuels and building materials are both delivered through a single hatch, so we'll give them both the same name: FUD.

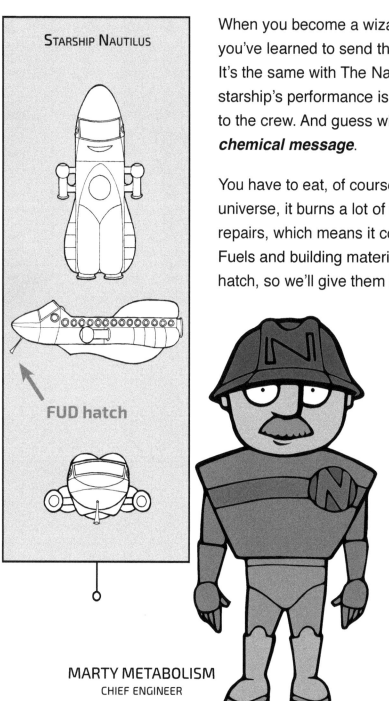

STARSHIP NAUTILUS

FUD hatch

MARTY METABOLISM
CHIEF ENGINEER

As the captain, you can choose what kind of FUD goes through the hatch. That's the good news. But once again, here's the not-so-good news: **you can't decide what The Nautilus will do with the FUD**. Those decisions are made by the ship's chief engineer — an absolutely amazing app we'll call Marty Metabolism, or just Marty for short.

Marty is probably the most important member of the entire crew. We'll let Dr. Fishbones explain why.

Marty's responsibilities are enormous. He's in charge of all the building and repair projects. He keeps the engines running. He controls the heating system. He monitors and manages the fuel supply. And he has to do all those jobs at the same time, every hour of every day. We couldn't do anything without him. He's amazing.

You may have heard that some people have a fast metabolism, while others have a slow metabolism. So what exactly does that mean?

I'll explain, Captain. Suppose The Nautilus lands on a cold planet with strong gravity, and Marty believes the ship is too heavy to take off again. The logical solution is to burn away some of the stored fuel. So he opens the windows to let in cold air, then turns up the heating system. He turns on all the lights and monitors. He orders his building crews to tear down and rebuild sections of the ship, using power tools that require energy. The ship is now burning fuel at a high rate, so we would say it has a fast metabolism.

Now suppose instead that Marty is concerned we won't have enough fuel to reach our next destination. So he closes the windows, turns off the lights and monitors, stops all the repair work, and turns the thermostat down to 60 degrees. When Dr. Fishbones complains of being cold, Marty gives him a big, ugly sweater to keep warm. The ship is now burning fuel at a much lower rate, so we would say it has a slow metabolism.

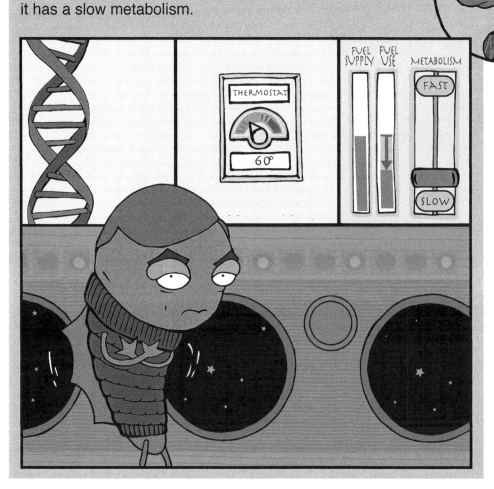

Your job as the captain would certainly be easier if you could just send orders directly to Marty, like this:

Unfortunately, that's not how The Nautilus was programmed. As an app, Marty doesn't know or care how you want him to do his job. He simply responds to what's happening inside the ship and to messages from the rest of the crew.

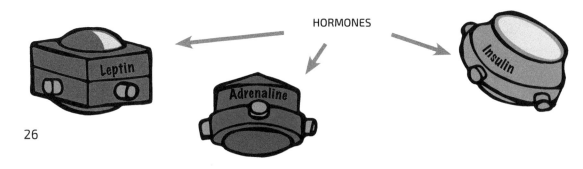

The Brain and the crew send alerts and commands to each other through chemical messengers called hormones. When Marty receives a message, it's often a command, such as **GET TALLER**, or **BUILD BIGGER MUSCLES**, or **STORE MORE FAT**.

To follow those commands, Marty has to adjust how much FUD the ship burns for energy, how much it stores as fat, and how much it converts into building materials. In other words, he has to adjust the difference between **calories in vs. calories out**.

That's why The Piggy Bank Theory doesn't work in real life. It assumes your metabolism stays the same unless you raise it by exercising. But in fact, Marty can speed up or slow down your metabolism quite a bit — and he will, depending on the messages he receives.

Here's an example: one of the instructions programmed into The Nautilus is to keep building a bigger ship for the first 15 to 20 years. So if you're not an adult yet, you're growing taller. To grow taller, you have to consume more FUD than you burn, then convert the leftover FUD into building materials.

If we applied The Piggy Bank Theory, we would explain growing taller like this:

Wow, wouldn't that be great? If you were on the short side, you could just keep eating and eating until you were nine feet tall, then go play in the NBA. But of course, that's not how it works.

Correct, Captain. The Nautilus grows taller because The Brain triggers what we call the **Get Taller!** program. This program sends chemical messages to Marty that instruct him to build bigger bones, muscles and organs. To make sure he has the extra building materials, Marty triggers what we call the **Get Hungry!** program. This program sends messages that instruct you, as the captain, to deliver more FUD through the hatch.

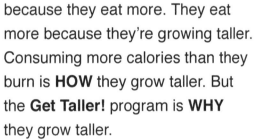

The **Get Taller!** program is the reason teenagers are known for their amazing appetites. They need the extra building materials to grow into their adult height. But they don't grow taller because they eat more. They eat more because they're growing taller. Consuming more calories than they burn is **HOW** they grow taller. But the **Get Taller!** program is **WHY** they grow taller.

> Teenagers don't grow taller because they eat more. They eat more because they're growing taller.

If you're still confused about calories and body size, think of it this way: suppose your dad is six-foot-five, and he's always complaining about having to squeeze himself into those stupid little seats on airplanes. To grow as tall as he is, your dad had to consume more calories than he burned. So according to the Piggy Bank Theory, you could avoid growing as tall as your dad by eating a little less than he did. Would that work?

Of course not. Like all important apps, Marty's code includes something called *redundancy*. That's a programmer's term that means if one block of code doesn't work, the program switches to another ... and another, and another, until the command is obeyed.

If your body is running the **Get Taller!** program and you decide to eat a little less, Marty will simply slow down your metabolism to burn less FUD for fuel. Then he'll convert the leftover FUD into building materials.

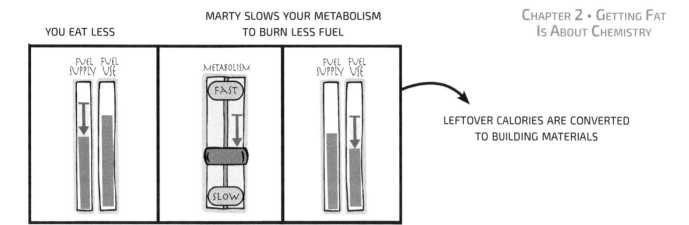

YOU EAT LESS

MARTY SLOWS YOUR METABOLISM
TO BURN LESS FUEL

LEFTOVER CALORIES ARE CONVERTED
TO BUILDING MATERIALS

That's what Marty is programmed to do. He follows commands by constantly adjusting how he uses calories.

That's why naturally lean people can eat 56,000 extra calories in eight weeks and barely gain any weight. That's why people like my wife weigh exactly the same, year in and year out, without ever thinking about calories. When they eat more, Marty speeds up their metabolisms to burn the extra calories. Their version of The Nautilus was programmed to avoid getting fat — and that's chemistry, not character.

Getting fat is also about chemistry. It begins when those chemical messengers called **hormones** tell Marty to run the **Get Fatter!** program and store more fat. It actually works a lot like the **Get Taller!** program ... but the extra calories are converted into fat instead of building materials. That's **WHY** you get fatter.

HORMONES

Since Marty is under orders to store more fat, he'll trigger the **Get Hungry!** program to make you eat more. But if that doesn't work, he'll slow down your metabolism to burn less fuel. Either way, you end up consuming more calories than you burn. That's **HOW** you get fatter.

The commands from hormones are so powerful, Marty can't just ignore them. Perhaps Mr. Spot can give us an example.

Certainly, Captain. In one experiment with rats, researchers performed a surgery that triggered the **Get Fatter!** program. The rats began eating in a manner you Earthlings would call "pigging out" and became very fat.

GET HUNGRY

RAT CHOW

FUEL SUPPLY FUEL USE

LEFTOVER CALORIES CONVERTED TO FAT

Aha, that must mean The Piggy Bank Theory is correct! The rats ate too many calories, and that's **WHY** they got fat.

That is incorrect, Captain. Later the researchers performed the same surgery on an identical group of rats, but did not allow them to eat more. Those rats became just as fat, just as quickly. Since they couldn't eat more, the rat version of Marty drastically slowed their metabolisms instead. Once again, they consumed more calories than they burned and became very fat. In both cases, it was the **Get Fatter!** program that made them fat.

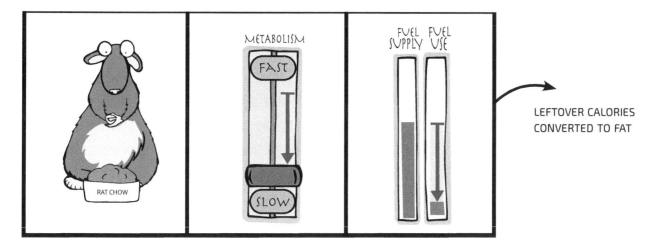

LEFTOVER CALORIES
CONVERTED TO FAT

The same thing can happen to people. A documentary I saw called *The Science of Obesity* featured a woman who was lean until about age 35. Then she suddenly started getting very fat. She cut her calories to just 1500 per day and still got fatter.

So, was she consuming more calories than she was burning? Yes, absolutely. That is always **HOW** we get fat. But was consuming too many calories **WHY** she got fat?

That is highly illogical, Captain. She was eating far less than most adults, but still gaining weight.

A doctor finally figured out **WHY** she kept getting fatter, Captain. She had a small tumor on her brain that was triggering the **Get Fatter!** program. Marty was under orders to store more fat, and he can't just ignore his orders. So every time she ate less, Marty responded by slowing down her metabolism.

If you're getting fat, I'm not suggesting you have a brain tumor. That's a very rare condition. But something in your body is telling Marty to run the **Get Fatter!** program. Consuming more calories than you burn isn't the cause of the problem. It's the result of Marty following his orders.

By now, you may be thinking to yourself, "Okay, I understand Marty can slow down my metabolism if I eat less. But if I keep cutting my calories, I have to lose weight eventually. After all, Marty can't slow the ship's fuel use down to nothing."

That's true. If you're willing to starve yourself, at some point Marty has to convert stored fat into fuel to prevent The Nautilus from shutting down. But starving yourself to become thin is a terrible idea, and it almost always fails in the long run.

If you watch shows like *The Biggest Loser*, you've seen people lose a lot of weight by starving themselves. But here's what *The Biggest Loser* didn't show you: most of the contestants were miserable the whole time, and most of them gained back all the weight after the show was over. As Mr. Spot can explain, that's no surprise.

Indeed, Captain. Studies conducted on former contestants from *The Biggest Loser* concluded that after starving themselves to lose weight, their metabolisms were permanently slower. As a result, they can gain weight on fewer calories than before.

So why does that happen? If we want to lose weight by starving ourselves, why won't Marty go along with the plan? The answer is that he's simply trying to protect The Nautilus.

I recently read a book called *The Happiness Hypothesis* in which the author (a psychologist named Jonathan Haidt) explains that your body is like an elephant. Your conscious mind — the part of you that thinks and makes plans — is like a rider on top of the elephant. The rider likes to think he's in control, and often it seems that he is. After all, he's telling the elephant where to go.

But what do you suppose would happen if the rider tried to steer the elephant into a forest fire? I'm sure you can guess: The elephant would panic and run the other way, and suddenly the rider would learn he's not in control after all.

It's the same with The Nautilus. Long before you became its captain, Nature designed and programmed your starship to survive. If there's one instruction coded into every living creature in the universe, it's this: DON'T STARVE. You may think it's a fine idea to go hungry for weeks on end to lose weight, but your body disagrees. When you fight your own body, you're going to lose.

As the captain, you can think and make plans, but you can't change the code that was written into your biological apps. Or as Dr. Haidt explained it, the rider cannot order the elephant around against its will.

Trying to lose weight by starving yourself is like trying to drag the elephant into a fire. The crew of The Nautilus doesn't know or care that you want to look better in a swimsuit. The crew only knows that the ship is breaking down and running out of fuel. So they send distress signals to Marty that say **Starvation Emergency! Fire up the survival program!**

Marty will crank up the **Get Hungry!** program to make you eat more. But if you don't, Marty will trigger other programs to help the Nautilus survive — and survival means keeping the reserve fuel tanks as full as possible. So depending on your version of Marty, he will:

1. Slow down your metabolism so The Nautilus burns less fuel.

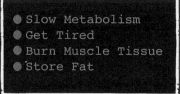

2. Release chemicals that make you feel tired and depressed so you don't waste fuel by flying around.

3. Break down your muscles and burn the muscle tissue for fuel.

4. Re-program the fuel system to make storing fat even easier than before — in order to survive the next **Starvation Emergency!**

Remember the mice who had their calories cut by five percent, but ended up with bigger fat cells? Their bodies interpreted less food as a **Starvation Emergency!** The mouse version of Marty responded by drastically reducing their fuel use and storing extra fat. In fact, he was so determined to store fat, he burned muscle tissue for fuel instead of fat. So the mice ended up with more fat and less muscle — all because cutting calories triggered the **Starvation Emergency!** program written into their biological code.

That's why advice based on The Piggy Bank Theory can completely backfire. You try starving yourself, but the crew keeps blasting hunger alerts, Marty slows down your metabolism, and soon the ship starts wobbling and breaking down. As the captain, you may not know exactly what's going wrong, but you know you feel miserable.

So you go back to eating just as much FUD as you did before ... but remember, Marty slowed down your metabolism to save fuel. So you not only gain back the weight you lost, there's a good chance you gain back more. You went from your normal diet, to a diet that made you feel hungry and cranky and tired, then back to your normal diet — and the result of all that misery is that you end up fatter than when you started.

And who do you blame? Probably yourself. Maybe with a little help from these guys.

If there's one thing I hope you understand after reading this book, it's this: if you tried to lose weight by following advice based on The Piggy Bank Theory and couldn't do it, **YOU didn't fail**. The advice failed. The diet failed. The Piggy Bank Theory failed. It failed because it's based on simple math that works fine and dandy with a piggy bank, but not with human biology — because that's not how our bodies are programmed.

The good news is that you can lose the extra weight. I've done it, despite spending most of my life as a fat guy, and so have millions of other people. But to burn away the fat and keep it off, you have to work *with* the code written into your body's chemistry, not against it. You have to stop firing up the **Get Fatter!** program. You have to stop triggering the **Get Hungry!** program when you shouldn't be hungry. And you absolutely, positively have to avoid triggering a **Starvation Emergency!**

Every time you eat, you send chemical messages to the crew of The Nautilus. What you eat — and don't eat — also determines which messages Marty sends back to you. If you're not happy with your starship, the only way to improve it is to change the messages that trigger the ship's code. It isn't about character. It's about chemistry.

So let's talk about food ... and why different foods trigger different programs inside The Nautilus.

3

STUFF I WISH I KNEW WHEN I WAS YOUR AGE:

HUNGER IS A MESSAGE FROM THE CREW

According to The Piggy Bank Theory, to lose weight, you simply have to eat less. If eating less means going hungry all the time, well, too bad. You just have to apply some discipline and put up with it.

As we've already seen, that's terrible advice. You don't lose weight and keep it off by going hungry. You lose weight and keep it off by changing **WHY** you're hungry in the first place.

When Marty Metabolism fires up the **Get Hungry!** program, he isn't trying to make you miserable or ruin your dream of wearing smaller pants. He's just trying to make sure the ship gets the fuel and materials it needs. That's one of his jobs as chief engineer.

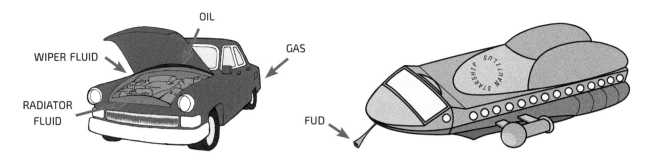

SEPERATE HATCHES FOR EVERYTHING A CAR NEEDS   ONE HATCH FOR EVERYTHING YOUR STARSHIP NEEDS

Unfortunately, figuring out what The Nautilus needs isn't as easy as figuring out what a car needs. A car has separate warning lights for gas, oil, wiper fluid and radiator fluid. There's also a separate hatch for delivering each one. If you see a warning light (and you're at least somewhat intelligent), you deliver the correct liquid through the correct hatch.

It would be cool if The Nautilus had four mouths — partly because you could sing your own harmonies — but that's not how it was designed. Everything your body needs has to be delivered through the FUD hatch. So the only way Marty can request a delivery is to run the **Get Hungry!** program.

That wasn't a problem when The Nautilus was designed and programmed. Back then, humans fed themselves by hunting, fishing and gathering wild plants. Everything in their diets was full of nutrients — that is, the fuels and materials The Nautilus was designed to use. The **Get Hungry!** program told people to eat, and the FUD they delivered through the hatch gave Marty what he needed.

Thousands of years later, our diets are completely different. Much of what we eat today is processed junk food. These products aren't even real foods. They're food-like substances. Yes, they can be quite tasty. But they make it easy to deliver a big load of FUD through the hatch without giving The Nautilus the nutrients it needs.

That creates a problem for Marty. Imagine if your father saw the low-oil light flashing on the dashboard of his car and responded by pouring gallons of Gatorade into the gas tank. Yes, he "fed" the car, but it still needs oil, so the warning light will continue flashing — and now the gas tank is full of the wrong fuel.

If your body is running the **Get Hungry!** program more often than it should, Marty is trying to tell you something. He's sending a message that says, *Captain, we need something down here! We need something we can only get from FUD, so make another delivery — pronto!*

Hunger is not your enemy. Hunger is a message. If you want to lose weight without starving and feeling miserable, you need to understand the message and make the right decisions about what to eat. That's your responsibility as the captain.

When we eat FUD, we deliver both large molecules and small molecules to The Nautilus. The large molecules are called macronutrients, and they come in three basic forms: proteins, carbohydrates and fats.

Proteins are Nature's building blocks. Fats, of course, are fats. Some are solid, and some are liquid. Liquid fats are called oils. Carbohydrates are sugar molecules strung together. We'll talk more about carbohydrates later.

PROTEINS   FATS   CARBOHYDRATES

The foods that are highest in protein come from animals: meats, eggs, milk and fish. Most plant foods also contain some protein, but not nearly as much. If you're hungry between meals, there's a good chance you're not eating enough protein. Mr. Spot will explain with an example.

In a scientific study, researchers gave one group of monkeys food that was high in protein. They gave a second group of monkeys food that had just as many calories per cup, but only half as much protein. The monkeys given the low-protein food ate twice as much. Not surprisingly, they also got fatter.

I see. And was that because they were bad little monkeys who didn't have any willpower?

Not at all, Captain. The monkeys given the low-protein food ate twice as much because the monkey version of Marty kept running the **Get Hungry!** program until they ate enough protein.

MAYBE YOU SHOULD TRY EATING A LITTLE LESS.

Once again, that's just Marty doing what he's been programmed to do. As chief engineer, Marty is constantly rebuilding and repairing the Nautilus to keep it from breaking down. Literally billions of times per day, he replaces old cells with new ones.

If you're not an adult yet, your ship is also running the **Get Taller!** program, which means Marty has to keep building bigger bones,

muscles and organs. That takes a lot of building materials —
and proteins are your body's primary building blocks. That's why
the word **protein** comes from the Greek word **proteios**, which
means **primary**.

Let me chime in here, Captain. As a doctor, I can tell you we
need protein for a lot more than just muscles and organs.
The hormones the crew uses to send messages are made
largely from protein. Vitamins and other nutrients are
delivered all over the ship in vehicles made from protein.

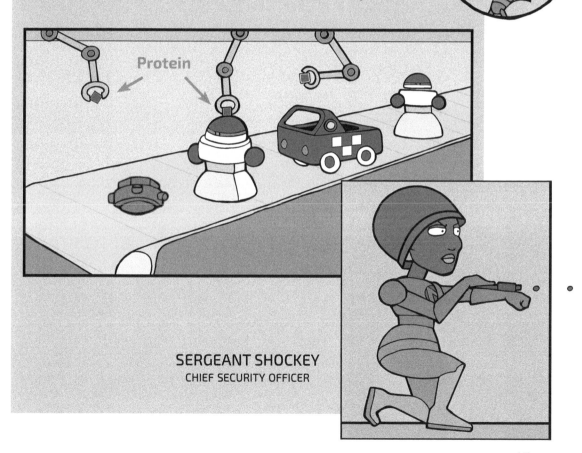

Protein

SERGEANT SHOCKEY
CHIEF SECURITY OFFICER

If The Nautilus is invaded by bacteria or other aliens, we call on Sergeant Shockey, our security officer, to battle the invaders. The soldiers and the weapons in her army are made from proteins. I could go on and on about —

Thank you, doctor, I'm sure you could. But I believe we've grasped the point: The Nautilus requires a lot of protein to function at a high level.

It certainly does. So what do you think happens when Marty runs the **Get Hungry!** program because he needs building materials, but you deliver a load of FUD that contains a teeny bit of protein and a whole lot of fuel?

Yup ... he's going to demand another delivery by firing up the **Get Hungry!** program all over again.

That's the bad news. The good news is that you can control your appetite naturally by eating more protein. We already saw that happen with monkeys, and science shows it works with humans too.

Indeed. In one study, for example, two groups of human volunteers were allowed to eat as much as they wanted. But one group was given foods higher in protein. On average, people in that group consumed 440 fewer calories per day. They weren't told to eat less, and they weren't counting calories. They ate less because they weren't as hungry.

They weren't as hungry because when Marty received the protein he needed, he stopped running the **Get Hungry!** program.

There's another reason eating more protein helps you lose weight: if Marty's afraid he'll run out of building materials, he cuts back on his building and repair projects. Slowing down those projects means slowing down your metabolism. But when you eat foods that are high in protein, Marty sees plenty of building materials coming through the FUD hatch. So even if you consume fewer calories, Marty is more likely to keep your metabolism high.

Proteins are the BIG building blocks for The Nautilus. But to build and maintain such a complicated ship, Marty and his construction crews also need plenty of smaller materials and lots of good tools. These small materials and tools are called micronutrients. You probably know them as vitamins and minerals. It would take an entire book to list the micronutrients The Nautilus needs and why it needs them. So let's ask Dr. Fishbones to give us a brief summary.

To build strong bones, Marty needs minerals like copper and calcium. To build hormones, he needs folate, iodine, and selenium. To build the blood cells that carry nutrients all over the ship, he needs iron. To build and repair cell walls, he needs choline and phosphorous. To maintain the

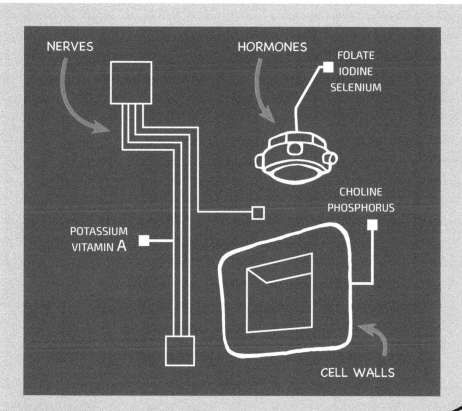

NERVES

HORMONES

FOLATE
IODINE
SELENIUM

CHOLINE
PHOSPHORUS

POTASSIUM
VITAMIN A

CELL WALLS

nerves that serve as the ship's electrical wiring, he needs potassium and vitamin A. To arm Sergeant Shockey's troops when they battle foreign invaders, he needs vitamins C and D. To convert FUD into fuel, he needs B vitamins and magnesium. I could go on and on about —

Thank you, doctor, I'm sure you could. But the captain asked for a brief summary, and I believe we've grasped the point: The Nautilus requires a lot of vitamins and minerals to function at a high level.

It sure does. Without those vitamins and minerals, the ship starts to break down. So once again, what do you think happens when Marty fires up the **Get Hungry!** program because he needs those small building materials and tools, but you deliver a load of FUD that's mostly fuel?

Yup ... he's going to demand another shipment by firing up the **Get Hungry!** program.

So just like with protein, science shows that eating food high in micronutrients helps to control your appetite naturally.

Indeed. In several studies, human volunteers who were given extra vitamins and minerals ended up eating less, even though they weren't told to eat less or count calories.

I guess that means the vitamins and minerals were big enough to fill their bellies.

No, Captain. As noted earlier, micronutrients are incredibly small. For example, to eat one pound of vitamin A, you'd need to eat a million pounds of broccoli.

That would be a very bad idea!

Yes, we know, Doctor. I was merely explaining that micronutrients are incredibly small, but also incredibly necessary. So when people don't consume sufficient micronutrients, Marty is likely to continue running the **Get Hungry!** program. If they do consume sufficient micronutrients, he's more likely to stop running the **Get Hungry!** program, as demonstrated in the study.

Once again, that's just Marty doing his job. If your goal is to lose weight, it's perfectly okay to eat a little less. But you have to give The Nautilus the nutrients it needs. You can't do that by eating food-like substances. Even when those products start out as nutritious foods, all that processing removes most of the nutrients. In other words, you can get a nice dose of potassium and vitamin C from a potato, but not from a bag of potato chips.

Food-like products can satisfy your appetite for awhile — but not because The Nautilus has what it needs. When the belly of the ship becomes full and begins to stretch, special sensors warn Marty to stop running the **Get Hungry!** program. But by the time that happens, you've probably consumed way more FUD than you actually need.

Marty has to do something with all that extra fuel. If you're one of those lucky people (like my wife), Marty will crank up your metabolism and burn it away. But if you're not so lucky, Marty will store the extra calories as fat. So just like with protein, to eat less without going hungry, you have to give The Nautilus what it needs. That means real, unprocessed foods that are high in nutrients, like these:

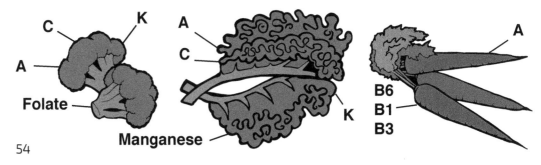

If you're like a lot of kids, you might be thinking, "But I don't like vegetables!" Well, I don't like vegetables either if they're just cooked and tossed on a plate. But I love them when they're mixed with the right kinds of fats. And despite what you may have heard, the right kinds of fats are good for you.

With all the anti-fat messages we've seen in the past 35 years, you'd think the quickest way to become healthy is to cut all the fat and cholesterol from your diet. But The Nautilus wasn't designed and programmed to run on a low-fat diet.

When Marty and his construction crews rebuild and repair The Nautilus, they use blocks of protein to give it strength. But to avoid damage, most of the ship's parts also have to be flexible. After all, you're a human being. You need to jiggle and wiggle and perhaps even dance.

Marty uses fat to make The Nautilus flexible. In fact, fat is the ship's second-most important building material.

Correct, Captain. Fat and cholesterol are required to construct hair, fingernails, lungs, nerves, and of course the skin that surrounds the ship. The super-computer we call **The Brain** is constructed mostly from fat. In fact, if someone removed all the fat and cholesterol from The Brain, it would shrink to one-third of its normal size. Speaking of which, perhaps Dr. Fishbones would like to list other ways The Nautilus uses fats.

Thank you, Spot. As you know, Captain, the ship's apps are triggered by messengers called **hormones**. Those hormones are made largely from fat and cholesterol. Many of the micronutrients we talked about earlier are what we call **fat-soluble**. That means to travel through the bloodstream, they have to be carried in a vehicle made from fat. Otherwise, they never reach the areas of the ship where they're needed.

Vitamin D has to travel in a vehicle made from fat. Vitamin A has to travel in a vehicle made from fat. Vitamin K has to travel in a vehicle made from fat. I could go on and on ...

Yes, Doctor?

Sorry, I was waiting for Spot to cut me off. Anyway, the bottom line is that The Nautilus needs quality fats to function at a high level. So if Marty doesn't get the fats he needs, he's going to keep running the **Get Hungry!** program.

I found that out the hard way. Back when the so-called experts were all recommending low-fat diets, I kept trying to live on low-fat and fat-free foods. I was hungry and miserable the whole time. When I started putting good quality fats like butter and olive oil back into my diet, a funny thing happened: I ended up eating less without feeling hungry. Mr. Spot can give us the scientific explanation of why that happened.

Certainly, Captain. When good fats are delivered through the FUD hatch, they trigger the release of a hormone called cholecystokinin, or CCK as we call it for short. CCK is one of the chemical messengers that tell Marty he can stop running the **Get Hungry!** program.

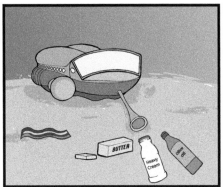 

Now that you've learned about the tools and building materials
The Nautilus needs to function properly, I hope you understand
why a diet based on The Piggy Bank Theory is such a bad idea.
If your body is running the **Get Hungry!** program too often, it
probably means Marty isn't getting what he needs. But according
to The Piggy Bank Theory, the cure is to simply eat less — which
means giving Marty ***even less of what he needs!***

How do you think he and the other crew members will react if
that happens? I'm sure you can guess. They'll send out distress
signals like crazy. Marty will run the **Get Hungry!** program non-
stop. You'd have to be super-human to resist — and if you did, it
would be a bad decision. You might lose a little weight, but The
Nautilus would start breaking down and you'd end up feeling
miserable.

So I'll say it again: you don't lose weight and keep it off by
going hungry. You lose weight by changing **WHY** you're hungry
in the first place. When your meals include enough protein,

micronutrients and quality fats, Marty stops running the **Get Hungry!** program. Then you eat less without even trying.

That's why I never have to worry about my daughters eating too much. They eat food that's high in the nutrients they need. They stop eating when they're not hungry anymore — often with food still on their plates.

4

HOW THE FUEL SYSTEM WORKS

As we just saw, Marty Metabolism will fire up the **Get Hungry!** program when The Nautilus needs protein, micronutrients, or good fats for building materials and tools. But of course, Marty also makes you hungry when the ship is low on fuel.

Yes, it's obvious that we need FUD for fuel. But the ship's fuel system is a lot more complicated than you might think.

When I was a kid, I thought our digestive systems work like the gas tank in a car. Fill the tank, and your body burns food for fuel. When the tank is nearly empty, the low-fuel light starts flashing and you get hungry again.

In fact, your body's fuel system is almost nothing like a car's. The Nautilus doesn't have just one fuel tank. It has lots of tanks, spread out all over the ship. Some of the tanks store sugar and some store fat. Those are the ship's two main fuels, and most of our cells can burn either one for energy. But to avoid damaging the entire system, The Nautilus **has to burn the right mix of fuels at exactly the right time**. Dr. Fishbones will explain why.

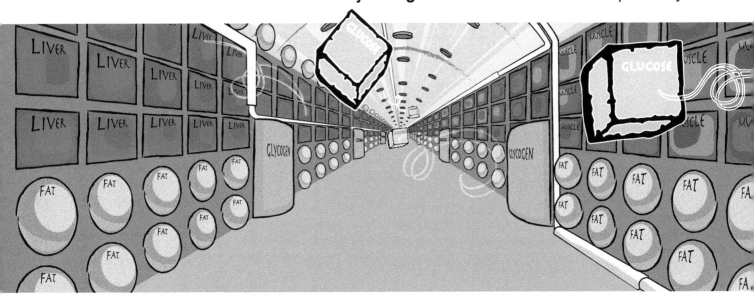

The super-computer we call **The Brain** is made mostly from fat. But to stay powered up, it absolutely, positively needs a steady supply of a sugar called glucose. Glucose travels through the bloodstream, which is why we doctors also call it blood sugar. Without glucose, The Brain will shut down — and then so will The Nautilus. So the ship's bloodstream must always contain some glucose.

But if there's too much glucose in the bloodstream, everything starts to break down. The hoses crack, the spark plugs misfire, the engine sputters, and the cells become damaged. The extra glucose starts sticking to parts of the ship and gumming up the works. To put it in medical terms, **high blood sugar is toxic**. Blood sugar will rise for a while after FUD is delivered through the hatch, and that's fine. But most of the time, there should only be about one teaspoon of glucose in the entire bloodstream.

As chief engineer, Marty has many important jobs. But controlling the mix of fuels the ship burns might be the most important. To protect The Brain, he can't let blood sugar go too low. To protect the rest of the ship, he can't let blood sugar go too high. So Marty is constantly monitoring the fuel supply and deciding whether to burn sugar and store fat, or burn fat and store sugar, or burn and store some of each.

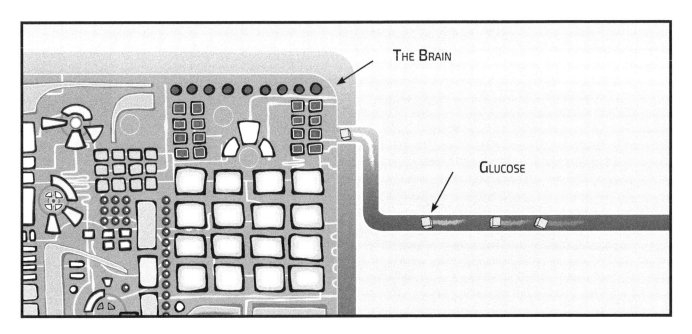

THE BRAIN

GLUCOSE

Marty's ability to handle this job is a fine example of how brilliantly The Nautilus was programmed. Let's take a look at how he does it.

Suppose you open the hatch and deliver a meal of scrambled eggs cooked in butter and potatoes fried in lard. That meal contains protein, fats, cholesterol and carbohydrates. The carbohydrates in the potato are in the form of **starch**. Starches are just bits of glucose bound together.

STARCHES
ARE CHAINS OF
GLUCOSE

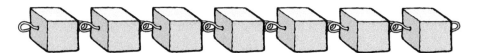

As always, Marty will use some of the FUD for fuel and some for building materials. But before any of the nutrients reach the bloodstream, they have to pass through tiny security filters that protect the ship. So before Marty can do anything with the FUD, a member of the Digestion Crew has to break it up into little bits. We'll call that crew member **Chef Chop-Chop**.

POTATO
(STARCHY CARBOHYDRATE)

Chop-Chop takes the protein from the eggs and slices it into little building blocks called amino acids. She chops the fats from the butter and lard into fatty acids. To process the potatoes, she has to break down the fibers and rip open the cells to release the starchy carbohydrates. Then she slices the starch into little bits of glucose.

EGG
(PROTEIN)
AMINO ACIDS

BUTTER & LARD
(FATS)
FATTY ACIDS

The bits of FUD that shouldn't go into the bloodstream continue moving through the digestive system and end up in the garbage chute. But the nutrients Chef Chop-Chop sliced into little bits slip through the security filters and into the bloodstream. That's where Marty takes over.

FIBER

SECURITY FILTER

GARBAGE CHUTE

BLOODSTREAM

Marty will probably set aside the cholesterol and most of the amino acids for building materials. Since fats are also an important building material, he'll set aside some fatty acids as well. But that still leaves more fuel in the bloodstream than The Nautilus can burn at the moment. So which does Marty burn first, the glucose or the fats?

Well, as Dr. Fishbones told us, **high blood sugar will damage The Nautilus**. So as glucose enters the bloodstream, Marty's first priority is to keep the blood sugar from going too high. That means he needs to burn the sugar for fuel — which also means he needs to store the fat. In other words, he needs to run the **Get Fatter!** program, at least for a little while. If possible, he also wants to remove some glucose from the bloodstream by storing it.

To accomplish all three tasks, Marty releases a hormone called **insulin**. Dr. Fishbones can explain what insulin does.

To put it simply, Captain, insulin's job is to push nutrients into cells. It pushes glucose into the muscle and organ cells, and they burn the glucose for fuel. At the same time, insulin pushes fat into the fat cells and closes the doors to keep the fat inside. That way, the ship continues burning glucose instead of fat. Finally, insulin pushes glucose into storage tanks called **glycogen stores**. Together, these actions lower the blood sugar after a new delivery of FUD.

INSULIN PUSHES GLUCOSE INTO MUSCLE AND ORGAN CELLS

INSULIN PUSHES FAT INTO FAT CELLS

INSULIN PUSHES GLUCOSE INTO GLYCOGEN STORES

If you read books or articles on nutrition, sooner or later you'll come across a so-called expert who says this: *Carbohydrates are your body's preferred source of energy!* We'll ask Mr. Spot to comment on that one.

That statement is based on a misunderstanding, Captain. In fact, the ship's muscles and many of its organs function better while burning fat. It's true that when the bloodstream is full of glucose and fats, the ship is programmed to burn the glucose first. But that's because Marty wants to lower the blood sugar to prevent damage, not because glucose is a better fuel. If there is alcohol in the bloodstream, it is burned for fuel before glucose — again, because alcohol can cause damage. Yet nobody would declare that alcohol is the preferred fuel for humans — although some of your human college students seem to believe it is.

So when blood sugar is high, Marty works the ship's controls to burn glucose and store fat. That's good, at least for a while. By burning away the blood sugar, Marty is protecting the ship from damage.

But as the blood sugar starts dropping, Marty has to adjust the fuel mix again. He can't let the blood sugar drop too low, because The Brain absolutely, positively needs a steady supply of glucose. So to save glucose for The Brain, Marty needs to switch most of the ship to burning fat instead.

To accomplish that task, Marty dials back the amount of insulin in the bloodstream. As insulin drifts away, the doors to the fat cells open up. Most parts of the ship prefer fat for fuel, so once fatty acids flow into the bloodstream, the cells begin burning fat. That saves the glucose for The Brain. Marty can also provide some extra glucose by opening up the glycogen stores.

FAT CELLS ARE A CRUCIAL PART OF THE SHIP'S FUEL SYSTEM

I hope you understand now that fat cells aren't just ugly piggy banks where The Nautilus dumps extra calories if you eat too much. Fat cells are a crucial part of the ship's fuel system. The Nautilus *needs* to store fat. By storing and releasing fatty acids at different times, Marty keeps the fuel mix exactly where it needs to be. That's why you can go for hours without eating and still feel energetic. Marty releases the fuel you need when you need it.

But at some point after your last meal, Marty decides it's best to stop draining fuel from the storage tanks. After all, allowing the fuel supply to drop too low is a danger to the ship. So he fires up the **Get Hungry!** program, and you deliver another load of FUD through the hatch. Then the whole process starts all over.

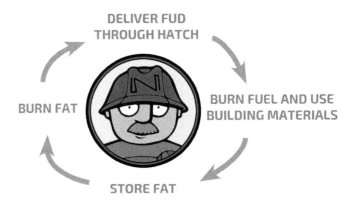

This is how The Nautilus was designed to work. Marty runs the **Get Hungry!** program just often enough to make sure you deliver the fuel and building materials he needs. After a meal, he runs the **Get Fatter!** program for a short time to store some fat. Then he shuts off the **Get Fatter!** program to release the fat. The fat cells grow large enough to serve their purpose in the fuel system, but not so large that they weigh down the ship.

Like I said, it's a fine example of brilliant programming. But as a programmer, I know that *apps are written to fit their environment.* If the environment changes, even the most brilliant app can produce bad results.

Here's an example: In the late 1990s, corporations had to spend billions of dollars to re-program software that stored dates like this:

$$01/15/18$$

We know the date is January 15, but what's the year? Well, the old software was programmed when the year was always 19-something. That was the environment. So the year would be 1918.

For several decades, that wasn't a problem. But when the year 2000 came around, the environment changed. Now the same software would produce bad results. If you were born in 2001 and someone entered your birthday as **01/15/01**, the software would assume you were already 100 years old. Imagine if that software also decided where you should live and what clothes you should wear.

We have a similar problem today with The Nautilus. The app that controls the fuel system worked perfectly for 99 percent of human history. That's because the app was programmed for an environment full of real foods. But since then, our food has changed so drastically, it's as if The Nautilus traveled to a completely different planet ... and then another, and another.

That's when The Nautilus began to break down far more often than it should.

5

TODAY'S "HEALTHY" DIET
ISN'T YOUR NATURAL DIET

A couple of years ago, my wife and I were at the grocery store and bumped into a woman whose son was in our daughter's class at school. We live in the South, which means when we see someone we know, we have to stop and chat, even if we're in a hurry. I believe it's a law. Naturally, the mommies talked about the kids.

The other mommy told us her son was getting fat, so she was going to make him play outside more often. I'm a nutrition nerd, so I couldn't resist peeking into her grocery cart. Here's some of what I saw:

Noodles, bread, cereal, skim milk, vegetable oil, skinless chicken breasts, a jug of apple juice.

Pretty much everything was labeled **Low-Fat!** or **Whole Grain!** When I saw those foods, I knew the other mommy's little boy wasn't going to lose weight by playing outside. If anything, I suspected he would keep getting fatter.

This mommy certainly meant well. She wasn't buying soda, or candy, or donuts, or Twinkies, or anything most people would call junk food. In fact, she was buying the foods many so-called experts tell us to eat.

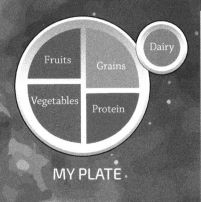

MY PLATE

If you're in school, you've probably been taught that these foods are good for you. You've probably been introduced to **MyPlate**, the guideline put out by the United States Department of Agriculture. (*The United States Department of Agriculture* is a mouthful, so from now on we'll just call it the **USDA**.)

This well-meaning mommy was apparently following the USDA's guidelines — and that's the problem. A low-fat diet based on grains doesn't help kids (or adults) lose weight. If anything, it's likely to make kids (and adults) even fatter. And worse, that diet can make kids (and adults) tired, cranky, hungry and sick. It simply isn't the diet The Nautilus was designed and programmed to handle.

For more than 99 percent of the time after its creation, The Nautilus lived on what we'll call **The Planet of Real Foods**.

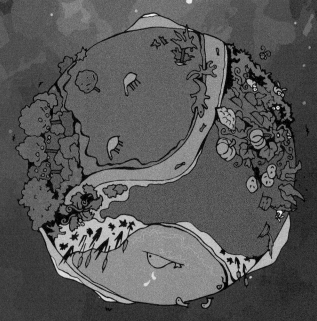

THE PLANET OF
REAL FOODS

Humans fed themselves by hunting, fishing and gathering plants like fruits, vegetables, nuts, roots and tubers. These foods are the natural human diet. After all, ancient humans didn't have machines to process food. So the natural foods for humans are the ones we can simply clean, cook and eat.

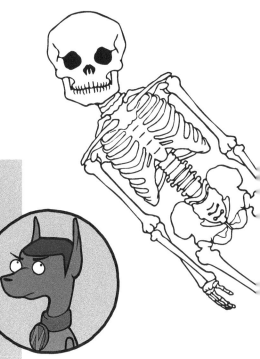

Scientists have learned quite a bit about ancient humans by studying two important sources of information: skeletons and poop. The poop tells us what they ate. The skeletons tell us about their health.

Indeed, Captain. Those skeletons show that ancient humans were tall, with thick bones. The bones show no signs of arthritis or other diseases that afflict modern humans. Most of the ancient humans also had straight teeth with no cavities.

Hmmm, they must have been really good about brushing and flossing.

That is incorrect, Captain. There were no drugstores back then, and nowhere to buy toothpaste, or a toothbrush, or dental floss. These humans had good teeth because the natural foods they consumed didn't harm their teeth.

These humans did NOT eat a low-fat diet. After a successful hunt, they ate the fattest part of the animal first. They gave extra fat and cholesterol to their growing children. They considered fat so important, they wouldn't hunt an animal unless it was fat enough to be valuable.

Some humans didn't leave The Planet of Real Foods until very recently. The Indians of the Great Plains, for example, fed themselves by hunting buffalo. According to what we're told today, all that fatty red meat should have made them fat. They should have had cancer and heart disease.

But they weren't fat or sick. American doctors described these Indians as the tallest, strongest, healthiest people they'd ever seen. They didn't become fat and sick until they were forced onto reservations and had to eat "civilized" foods, like flour made from wheat. To the Indians, those foods probably seemed like they came from another planet. And in a way, they did.

Several thousand years ago, humans in some parts of the world learned how to grow wheat and other grains. Over time, that caused a mass migration to **The Planet of FUD Farms**. The good news is that farmers could grow so much food, most people could do something else. That allowed civilization to develop.

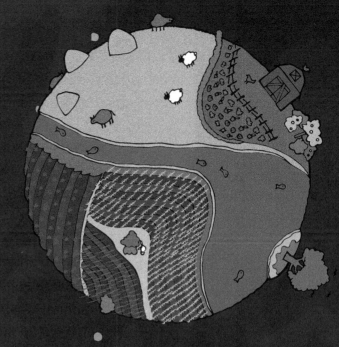

The bad news is that wheat and other grains aren't the foods The Nautilus was designed to handle. Once again, scientists know what happened on The Planet of FUD Farms because of skeletons, and from mummies discovered in Egypt.

Indeed, after humans began living on grains, they shrunk by nearly six inches. It took thousands of years for humans to return to their original height. Their bones also became thinner. They developed cavities and arthritis. Mummies found in ancient Egypt show that humans began dying of heart disease and cancer. An anthropologist named Jared Diamond called the switch to farming "quite possibly the worst mistake in human history."

Well, I don't know about that. Farms created civilization. Without civilization, I wouldn't be writing this book and you wouldn't be reading it. We'd both be busy hunting and gathering food. We wouldn't have televisions, airplanes, factories, automobiles, art galleries ... or people going to concerts and spending the entire time checking social media on their phones.

Migrating to The Planet of FUD Farms wasn't good for the health of The Nautilus. But things got even worse when many people migrated to **The Planet of Industrial FUD**.

On this strange new planet, humans started processing food with industrial machines. They began eating food-like products sold in boxes and bags. They created margarines and cooking oils by using chemicals to extract oil from soybeans, cotton seeds and corn. Sugar became a common ingredient in FUD. So did white flour made from wheat. Before industrial processing, those were expensive treats only rich people could afford.

THE PLANET OF
INDUSTRIAL
FUD

Around a hundred years ago, a dentist named Weston A. Price traveled around the world to study how living on The Planet of Industrial FUD was affecting The Nautilus. Everywhere he went, he saw the same thing: as people began eating more food-like products, their health got worse. They ended up with cavities and crooked teeth. They developed diabetes, heart disease and cancer — diseases that rarely afflicted the older folks who grew up eating real food.

Fortunately, most people still ate more real food than industrial food. Take a look at this poster:

That's the diet the U.S. government recommended in the 1940s. Eggs, butter, meat and whole milk were labeled as "protective foods" — which they are. People were told to eat just two servings of starchy foods each day. So if one of your starchy foods was a potato, you'd end up eating just one serving of bread or cereal.

This is how people ate in previous generations — and those people looked pretty good. Nobody was talking about an obesity epidemic back in those days. People weren't developing diabetes at a record rate, either.

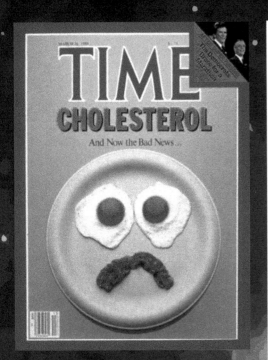

But then came perhaps the biggest mistake of all: a mass migration to **The Planet of the Preposterous Pyramid**. On this alien planet, magazines warned people that bacon and eggs would kill them because of the natural fats and cholesterol.

So instead of eating eggs, people ate industrial egg substitutes. Instead of eating butter, they ate butter substitutes made from industrial oils. Instead of putting cream in their coffee, they used artificial creamers full of sugars and chemicals. Instead of eating meats and other natural foods, they ate low-fat industrial foods full of soy, wheat and other grains.

On this crazy planet, we were told that the foods humans had been eating forever are bad for us. We were told that to be healthy, we need to eat grains and industrial oils that *no humans ever ate when The Nautilus was designed and programmed*. It makes absolutely no sense ... and yet we believed it. So we started eating more food-like products that only exist because of modern industry.

THE PLANET OF THE
PREPOSTEROUS PYRAMID

As a result, the brilliant programming that made The Nautilus such a fabulous ship is no longer operating in the environment it was designed to handle. Now our biological code is responding to chemical messages from FUD we were never meant to eat. Those messages are causing our starships to run the **Get Hungry!** and **Get Fatter!** programs too often, and for too long.

So if The Planet of the Preposterous Pyramid is such a lousy place, how did we end up here?

6

HOW BAD SCIENCE CAUSED A MASS MIGRATION TO THE WRONG PLANET

The mass migration to The Planet of the Preposterous Pyramid was driven by two powerful forces that often dominate our part of the universe: bad science and bad politics.

You need to understand why the science was bad. So before we continue the story of the migration, let's take a brief detour through Mr. Spot's part of the universe and talk about science.

Let's suppose Dr. Fishbones visits a tiny world called **The Planet of Tragic Fashions** and gathers a bunch of data on all the residents. When he runs that data through a computer, he notices a surprising connection.

Captain! I've discovered that residents who get just-above-the-butt tattoos are more likely to develop cancer! We've got to put a stop to those tattoos, Captain!

Is Dr. Fishbones correct? Do his findings prove that the tattoos are causing cancer?

That would be incorrect, Captain. Dr. Fishbones conducted what's called an observational study. In an observational study, we look for traits and behaviors that seem to occur in the same people. We may notice for example, that people who play basketball are often very tall. So we could say playing basketball is linked to being tall. We might also say basketball is correlated or associated with being tall.

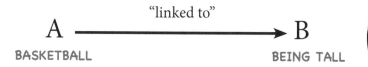

A ———"linked to"———> B

BASKETBALL   BEING TALL

But it would be illogical to conclude that playing basketball makes people taller. As Dr. Fishbones should know, just because a behavior and a result are linked, it doesn't mean the behavior causes the result. Just-above-the-butt tattoos may be "linked" to cancer, but it could simply be that people who get tattoos are more likely to smoke. Or drink large sodas. Or play with toxic chemicals. These other factors are what we scientists call confounding variables.

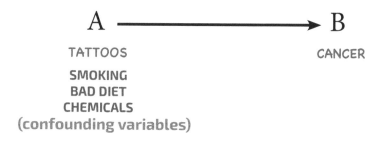

A ————————————> B

TATTOOS   CANCER

SMOKING
BAD DIET
CHEMICALS
(confounding variables)

Most studies on diet and health are observational studies — and observational studies are full of confounding variables. To make matters worse, researchers gather data on what people eat by sending out surveys that look like this:

Over the last 12 months, how often did you consume:

Whole milk (4%), NOT in coffee, NOT on cereal: Never I 1-6 per year I 7-11 per year I 1 per month I 2-3 per month I 1-2 per week I 3-4 per week I 5-6 per week I 1 per day I 2-3 per day I 4-5 per day I 6+ per day. Portion size: less than 1/2 cup I 1/2 to 1 cup I more than 1 cup.

Breads or dinner rolls, NOT INCLUDING ON SANDWICHES: Never I 1-6 per year I 7-11 per year I 1 per month I 2-3 per month I 1-2 per week I 3-4 per week I 5-6 per week I 1 per day I 2-3 per day I 4-5 per day I 6+ per day. Portion size: less than 1 slice or roll I 1 or 2 slices or rolls I more than 2 slices or rolls.

Ground beef in mixtures such as tacos, burritos, meatballs, casseroles, chili, meatloaf: Never I 1-6 per year I 7-11 per year I 1 per month I 2-3 per month I 1-2 per week I 3-4 per week I 5-6 per week I 1 per day I 2-3 per day I 4-5 per day I 6+ per day. Portion size: less than 3 ounces I 3 to 7 ounces I more than 7 ounces.

So, how many ounces of ground beef did you eat last year? You have no idea, right? Neither do the people who answer the questions. So they guess. But their guesses end up in observational studies that are reported in the media as if they prove something. They don't. That's why you'll open a newspaper or visit a news site one week and see a headline like this ...

... then some weeks later, you'll see a headline like this:

Those are real headlines, by the way. To most people, it seems as if those darned scientists can't make up their minds about which foods are good for us. But that's what happens with observational studies — because they don't prove anything.

In fact, a researcher named Dr. John Ioannidis reviewed decades of research and found that 80 percent of the conclusions drawn from observational studies turned out to be wrong. That means observational studies are worthless.

> Not entirely, Captain. On my planet, when observational studies lead to scary headlines, we take the newspaper and use it to paper-train our puppies ... I mean, children.

If you're in school, you may have been introduced to **The Scientific Method**, which looks like this:

The Scientific Method

1. Gather accurate data and make observations.

2. Based on the data, form a **hypothesis**. (A **hypothesis** is just a possible explanation of what we observed.)

3. Test the hypothesis by conducting a carefully controlled experiment.

4. Gather accurate data from the experiment.

5. Based on a careful and thorough analysis of the data, reach a conclusion.

The results of experiments must be consistent. If other scientists find different results, we must conclude that our hypothesis is wrong.

As you can see, an observational study only gets us to step two. To complete all five steps, scientists conduct what's called a **clinical study**. Once again, Mr. Spot will explain.

In a **clinical study**, Captain, we divide people into large groups that are balanced for factors like age, gender, and current health habits. Then we make a small change in one group and see what happens. To test what Dr. Fishbones believes, the small change would be giving the subjects in one group a just-above-the-butt tattoo.

So, let's suppose Dr. Fishbones brings in a tattoo artist and conducts that study ...

After the five-year study period, Captain, people in both groups had virtually identical rates of cancer. This means the hypothesis promoted by Dr. Fishbones is not valid. These tattoos are unattractive, but they do not cause cancer.

And I bet you're just *soooo* happy about that, aren't you, Spot?

I wouldn't know, Doctor. My species doesn't feel emotions.

So after that brief detour through the universe of science, let's return to the story of how bad science caused a mass migration to the wrong planet.

In the 1950s, a scientist named Ancel Keys launched an idea that would change our part of the universe forever. The idea was called the **Diet-Heart Hypothesis**, which looks like this:

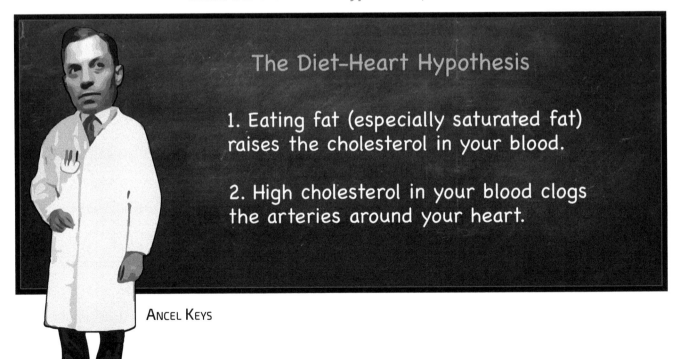

The Diet-Heart Hypothesis

1. Eating fat (especially saturated fat) raises the cholesterol in your blood.

2. High cholesterol in your blood clogs the arteries around your heart.

ANCEL KEYS

Most people these days believe the Diet-Heart Hypothesis is based on good science. But when Keys first presented his hypothesis at a scientific convention, almost nobody was impressed. Doctors, scientists, and even the American Heart Association didn't find Keys very convincing — and with good reason. Mr. Spot will explain:

Certainly, Captain. Keys based his hypothesis on an observational study. After gathering a small amount of data in just a handful of countries, he noticed that in countries where people ate more saturated fat, more people died of heart disease. But as we've seen, observational studies are often wrong and are full of confounding variables.

For example, in the countries where people ate more fat, they also ate more sugar. They exercised less. They ate fewer vegetables. In other words, Captain, there were major weaknesses in his observational study. It didn't prove anything.

It would be nice if all scientists were like Mr. Spot and only interested in finding the truth. But in our world, scientists are just like other people. Some of them have big egos and want to be right — no matter what the evidence says. So when his ideas were rejected by other scientists, Ancel Keys responded by starting the scientific version of an intergalactic war.

He fired off paper after paper, trying to destroy any scientists who disagreed with him. He gathered a small band of allies and took control of the American Heart Association. After that, the Heart Association began putting its stamp of approval on all kinds of "healthy" low-fat foods ... like Cocoa Puffs.

Other scientists fought back with clinical studies — the kind that actually matter. And as Mr. Spot can tell you, those studies concluded that the Diet-Heart Hypothesis is wrong.

In several studies, Captain, people who went on low-fat diets had just as many heart attacks as people who didn't. In two studies, people who switched from saturated fats to vegetable oils actually had more heart attacks. This should lead us to conclude that saturated fats do not cause heart disease — assuming we're being logical, of course.

In a fair battle for truth, the Diet-Heart Hypothesis would have been shot down and ended up on The Planet of Debunked Ideas. But the battle wasn't fair ... because in the end, the Diet-Heart Hypothesis was rescued by an ally so powerful, even the best scientists couldn't fight back: the United States government.

In the late 1970s, a government committee headed by Senator George McGovern decided it should tell the American people what to eat. McGovern was on a low-fat diet at the time and believed everyone else should be too. So the hearings went something like this:

That's right ... Americans were told to switch to a low-fat, low-cholesterol diet because a politician decided we couldn't wait for all the evidence to come in.

Once the government joined sides with the Diet-Heart Hypothesis, a lot of scientists found out the hard way it's not a good idea to disagree with the overlords.

To be fair, not all scientists who disagreed with the Diet-Heart Hypothesis were intimidated. Some were simply ignored ... including scientists who worked for the government.

Soon after the McGovern committee's hearings, the USDA told one of its scientists to write new dietary guidelines. After a lot of careful research, she wrote a report recommending a diet that looked pretty much like this.

Does that look familiar? It's the same diet the government recommended in the 1940s. It wasn't a low-fat diet, and it included just two servings of starchy foods per day.

But when the scientist sent her recommendations to the government overlords for review, she got the surprise of her life.

Yup. The USDA ignored her advice and came up with **The Food Pyramid**, which told people to eat six to 11 servings of grains per day. The scientist believed eating all that grain could turn people into fat diabetics, so she asked some important questions — such as "WHAT THE HECK JUST HAPPENED?!"

What happened is that the USDA got into the diet-advice business. But the USDA's job isn't to make us healthy. The USDA's job is to sell grains.

In the United States, crops like corn and wheat are subsidized, meaning the government pays farmers to grow them. So that's what our farmers grow — lots and lots of grains. Those grains end up being processed into countless food-like products.

Some of the richest and most powerful companies in the world are in the industrial-food business. They use their money and power to help politicians get elected. They get their own people appointed to positions at the USDA. They give money to university nutrition programs and to organizations like The American Heart Association.

That's how the mass migration to The Planet of the Preposterous Pyramid began. After ignoring the real science, the USDA told us migrating away from real foods like butter and eggs would make us healthier. So did organizations that get most of their money from the makers of industrial FUD. We believed them.

But living on The Planet of the Preposterous Pyramid isn't good for you or The Nautilus. It's good for companies that sell industrial FUD. On this crazy planet, you buy their food-like products. You eat the processed grains the U.S. government pays farmers to grow — exactly what the USDA wants.

If the overloads at the USDA had simply suggested we migrate to The Planet of the Preposterous Pyramid, maybe things wouldn't have turned out so bad. But they insisted. They ordered all government facilities to follow their advice, including schools. That's why your school lunch is probably low-fat, with lots of grains, and almost no flavor.

97

The good news is that there's been a revolution in the universe. For three decades, nearly all the information about diet and health was controlled by the overlords at the USDA and a small group of their allies. But when the internet exploded into cyberspace, the overlords could no longer control the flow of information. Rebel doctors and researchers began sharing their findings with the entire universe. Newspapers, magazines and scientific journals no longer believed everything the overlords said about diet and health.

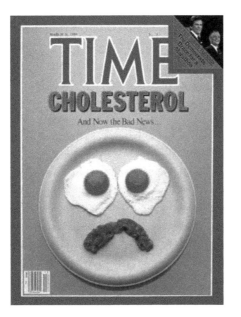

In 1984, *TIME* magazine encouraged the migration to The Planet of the Preposterous Pyramid by declaring that fat and cholesterol can kill us. In 2015, they declared that the "experts" got it all wrong. Now they tell us to eat butter.

Format: Abstract ▾

J Am Coll Cardiol. 2004 Mar 3;43(5):731-3.

The diet-heart hypothesis: a critique.

Weinberg SL[1].

⊕ Author information

Abstract
The low-fat "diet-heart hypothesis" has been controversial for nearly 100
vigorously by the National Cholesterol Education

SCIENTIFIC
AMERICAN.

SUBSCRIBE

English ▾ Cart Si

**Carbs against Cardio: More
Evidence that Refined
Carbohydrates, not Fats, Threaten
the Heart**

Whether the new thinking will be reflected in this year's revision of the federal dietary
guidelines remains unclear

No link found between saturated fat and heart disease

Cambridge University academic have looked over previous studies on
saturated fat and discovered there is no link to heart disease

f 26K   ⭕   📌 107   in 119   ⬛ 26K   ✉ Email

MEDICAL EXAMINER HEALTH AND MEDICINE EXPLAINED. MARCH 25 2010 1:02 PM

End the War on Fat
It could be making us sicker.
By Melinda Wenner Moyer

Thirty years ago, America declared war
against fat. The inaugural edition of
Dietary Guidelines for Americans, published
in 1980 and subsequently updated every
five years, advised people to steer clear of
"too much fat, saturated fat, and
cholesterol," because of purported ties
between fat intake and heart disease. The
message has remained essentially the

The New York Times

Study Questions Fat and Heart Disease Link

By ANAHAD O'CONNOR   MARCH 17, 2014 5:00 PM   💬 482

Many of us have long been told that saturated fat, the type found in
meat, butter and cheese, causes heart disease. But a large and

More and more scientists these days are declaring that the Diet-Heart Hypothesis was never based on good science. Senator McGovern said he couldn't wait for the evidence to come in — but now it has come in, and it shows that migrating to The Planet of the Preposterous Pyramid was a huge mistake.

Now that you know how we got here, let's look at why you need to leave this crazy planet.

7

STUFF I WISH I KNEW WHEN I WAS YOUR AGE:

How the Wrong FUD
Sends the Wrong Message

The Nautilus was programmed to choose the right fuels and building materials automatically. Inside the FUD hatch, special sensors send messages to The Brain that say *This is what the ship needs*. You experience those messages as **This Tastes Good**.

When humans hunted and gathered their food, this app worked perfectly. Our taste for sweets told us to eat fruits and sweet-tasting vegetables like carrots and squashes. Our taste for fats told us to eat olives, nuts, eggs and meats. Our taste for salts told us to eat meats and seafood. Our taste for spices told us to eat plants that were full of vitamins and minerals.

But as we've seen, apps are designed for a particular environment. The **This Tastes Good** app was programmed for The Planet of Real Foods. It still worked reasonably well when we migrated to The Planet of FUD Farms. But when we migrated to The Planet of Industrial FUD, we created a huge mismatch between the app and the FUD in the environment.

The makers of food-like products understand exactly how the **This Tastes Good** app works. So they add just the right combinations of sweet, fatty, salty and spicy flavors to industrial FUD. When these food-like products enter the FUD hatch, our sensors tell us *This Tastes Good. This is what the ship needs.* That's how The Nautilus was programmed.

But of course, these foods don't provide the fuels and building materials the ship needs. Worse, they send the wrong messages to Marty and the rest of the crew.

Wrong Message: Refined Carbohydrates

On the Planet of Real Foods, we gathered fruits and vegetables that grew above the ground. We dug into the ground for root vegetables like carrots and turnips. We also dug up tubers like potatoes and yams. These foods contain fiber, and the carbohydrates are locked inside plant cells.

So when these foods are delivered through the hatch, Chef Chop-Chop has plenty of work to do. To convert these foods into glucose, she first has to break down the fibers. Then she has to rip open the cells to release the carbohydrates.

That's exactly how Marty likes it. The glucose enters the bloodstream a little at a time, which makes it easy for him to monitor and adjust the fuel mix. As the blood sugar rises, he can switch to burning a bit more glucose and storing a bit more fat. The blood sugar stays exactly where he wants it: not too high, and not too low.

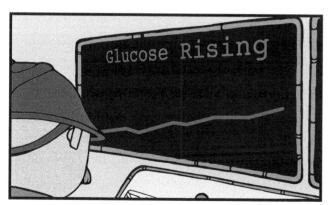
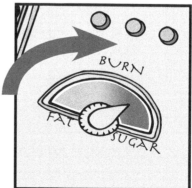

But when we migrated to The Planet of Industrial FUD, we began eating **refined carbohydrates**. **Refined** means the FUD is processed by machines that strip away the fibers and smash the plant cells. The stuff that's left over is called **acellular carbohydrate**, which means **no cells**. These refined starches are then processed into all kinds of food-like products: breads, cereals, pastries, noodles, cookies, crackers, chips, and hundreds of crunchy snacks.

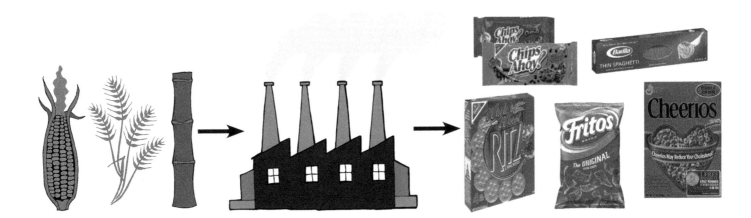

Decades ago, these refined starches were considered treats, not real food. Your great-grandmother would have told you refined starches are fattening. But on The Planet of the Preposterous Pyramid, we were told these food-like products are good for us. The USDA told us to eat six to 11 servings of these foods per day. The American Heart Association put its stamp of approval on countless boxes of refined starches — because they're low in fat.

These food-like products are tasty because they're designed to be tasty. But they create a huge problem for Marty — and for The Nautilus.

When you deliver refined carbohydrates through the hatch, there's not much for Chef Chop-Chop to do. There are no fibers to break down and no cells to rip open. So in almost no time at all, she slices the carbohydrates into glucose and dumps it all into the bloodstream. That creates an emergency for Marty.

When the blood sugar shoots up, Marty doesn't know how high it will go. He only knows he has to bring it down quickly, because high blood sugar will damage The Nautilus. So he does what he's been programmed to do: he fires up the **Get Fatter!** program and floods the bloodstream with insulin to force the ship to burn glucose instead of fat.

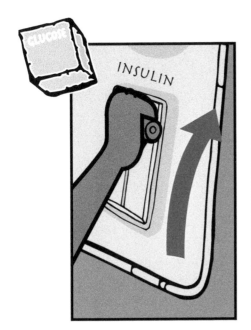

That solves the immediate problem, but creates another one. When insulin floods the system, it drives down blood sugar — sometimes too quickly. Normally, as blood sugar falls, Marty switches back to burning fat to preserve glucose for The Brain. He also releases glucose from the glycogen stores. But when the bloodstream is full of insulin, it closes the doors on both the fat cells and the glycogen stores.

Now the entire ship has a problem: there's not enough fuel in the bloodstream, and the storage tanks are closed. Pretty soon, The Brain can't process instructions efficiently and the ship starts to wobble. Meanwhile, Marty is receiving **LOW FUEL** alerts from all over The Nautilus.

So once again, he does what he's been programmed to do: he fires up the **Get Hungry!** program to demand another delivery of FUD. You shouldn't be hungry again, but you are — because the refined carbohydrates created a fuel emergency.

I see that happen to people all the time. They have a sandwich and chips for lunch, and two hours later they're hungry for candy or popcorn — because despite eating plenty of calories, they're storing too much fuel and their blood sugar is dropping. So they eat more food that spikes their blood sugar, and the whole pattern starts all over again.

Wrong Message: Refined Sugar

On The Planet of Real Foods, the sweet foods were fruits. That's because fruits contain a sweet-tasting sugar called **fructose**. But the fruits humans gathered in the wild were also full of micronutrients and fiber. To deliver a big load of fructose through the hatch, you'd have to eat more fruit than your belly could handle.

YOU'D HAVE TO EAT **65** STRAWBERRIES TO CONSUME
AS MUCH FRUCTOSE AS IN A CAN OF COLA

On The Planet of Industrial FUD, we can get our fructose from white table sugar or high-fructose corn syrup. These refined sugars are in all kinds of modern FUD: candies, desserts, cereals, pastries, crackers, salad dressings, sauces, yogurts, canned fruits and even breads. To make matters worse, we drink big servings of fructose in sodas and fruit juices.

The Nautilus was programmed to handle whole fruits, but not these big loads of refined fructose. Perhaps more than anything else we eat, they trigger the **Get Fatter!** program too often and for too long.

When you deliver real foods through the hatch, the fibers and nutrients trigger messages that tell Marty the ship has what it needs. So he stops running the **Get Hungry!** program and you feel full.

Refined sugars don't trigger those messages. That's why people can drink a large soda, then another, then another. Then they'll go eat a big meal — because despite drinking all those calories, they don't feel full.

GLUCOSE

In some lucky people, Marty will burn away the extra calories by cranking up the metabolism. But most of us aren't so lucky. So where do the calories go? Let's have Dr. Fishbones explain.

FRUCTOSE

White sugar and high-fructose corn syrup are both about half glucose and half fructose. We already saw the problem with refined glucose: Chef Chop-Chop dumps it all in the bloodstream, which creates a blood-sugar emergency for Marty.

But frankly, Captain, the refined fructose is even worse. The Nautilus can't store fructose in the glycogen stores. So the extra fructose goes to The Liver, the ship's conversion factory. The Liver converts the fructose to fat and stores it. This is a very bad place to store fat, because—

Thank you, Doctor, but before we discuss The Liver, I must interrupt to make another point: refined sugars are, of course, bad for The Nautilus. But they're even worse when combined with fats. The high blood sugar forces Marty to store fat at exactly the time fat is being delivered through the hatch. Meanwhile, the excess fructose is also being converted to fat. So the combination of refined sugar and fat essentially triggers two versions of the **Get Fatter!** program at the same time.

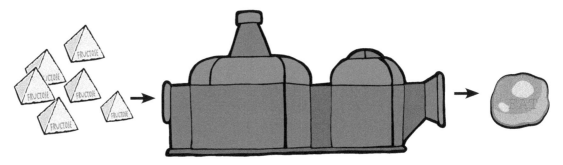

THE **LIVER** CONVERTS EXCESS **FRUCTOSE** INTO FAT

Yup. That's why getting fatter isn't just about how many calories you eat. It's also about which foods trigger the **Get Fatter!** program and how long they keep it running.

A trainer and health writer named Sam Feltham demonstrated that by running an interesting experiment on himself. Sam is one of those lucky people who doesn't gain weight easily.

So for 21 days, he ate more than 5,000 calories per day. But he got those calories from real foods: meats, eggs, nuts, and lots of vegetables. After all those extra calories, he gained less than three pounds. But his waist shrunk by nearly an inch, which means he gained some muscle and lost some fat.

For the second half of the experiment, he once again ate more than 5,000 calories per day for 21 days. But this time, he got a lot of the calories from refined sugars and starches: breads, cereals, pizza, candies and sugary sodas. The difference was amazing. He gained 16 pounds and got fatter around the waist.

Same guy, same number of calories per day, but a completely different result. When Sam ate real food, his version of Marty responded by cranking up his metabolism. But when he ate food-like products full of refined sugars and grains, Marty had to run the **Get Fatter!** program to deal with all those blood-sugar emergencies. So Sam got fatter.

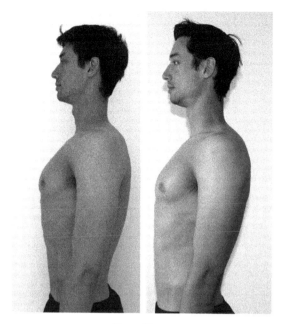

REAL FOOD

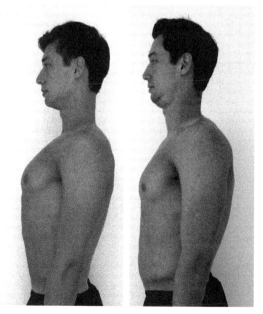

INDUSTRIAL FUD

Wrong Message: Too Many Carbohydrates For Your Version of The Nautilus

After The Nautilus was designed, humans migrated all over the world. In each new environment, The Nautilus was slowly reprogrammed to thrive on the FUD that was available. So the diet that's ideal for you partly depends on where your ancestors lived.

In warmer parts of the world, people gathered more fruits and starchy foods like tubers. In colder parts of the world, they relied more on hunting and fishing, because fewer plant foods were available. These different diets created slightly different versions of The Nautilus.

All versions of The Nautilus include a bit of biological code called the **AMY1 gene**. But some versions of The Nautilus have just one copy of the AMY1 gene, while others have up to 15 copies. As Mr. Spot can explain, that makes a big difference in how starchy foods affect the fuel system.

Indeed. Studies show that when people with several copies of the AMY1 gene consume starchy foods, they experience a slow and gentle rise in blood sugar. But when people with fewer copies of the AMY1 gene eat starchy foods, their blood sugar rises quickly and stays high longer.

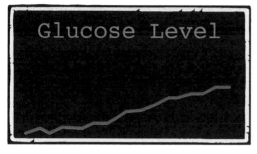

MORE COPIES OF AMY1 GENE

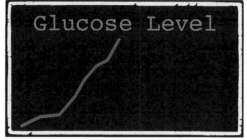

FEWER COPIES OF AMY1 GENE

I've seen that difference in my own family. As an experiment, I once ate a small bowl of spaghetti with no sauce. Afterwards, my blood sugar rose to 175, which is too high. My naturally thin wife ate the same-sized serving of spaghetti *and a potato*. Her blood sugar only rose to 115. That's probably part of the reason she's naturally thin. Right, Mr. Spot?

Correct, Captain. One study compared people with fewer than four copies of the AMY1 gene to people with more than nine copies. The people with fewer than four copies were eight times more likely to be obese.

In societies where people fed themselves by hunting, fishing and gathering plants, only 20 to 40 percent of the calories came from carbohydrates. And of course, those carbohydrates weren't refined. But on The Planet of the Preposterous Pyramid, we were all told to cut the fat and get 60 percent of our calories from grains and other carbohydrates. For most adults, that's more than 300 grams of carbohydrate per day.

Nutrition Facts

Serving Size 4 brussels sprouts (84g)

Amount Per Serving

Calories 40	Calories from Fat 5

% Daily Value*

Total Fat 0.5g	1%
Saturated Fat 0g	0%
Trans Fat 0g	
Cholesterol 0mg	0%
Sodium 25mg	1%
Total Carbohydrate 6g	2%
Dietary Fiber 3g	12%
Sugars 2g	
Protein 2g	

Vitamin A 8%	•	Vitamin C 120%
Calcium 2%	•	Iron 0%

*Percent Daily Values are based on a 2,000 calorie diet. Your daily values may be higher or lower depending on your calorie needs:

		Calories:	2,000	2,500
Total Fat	Less than		65g	80g
Saturated Fat	Less than		20g	25g
Cholesterol	Less than		300mg	300mg
Sodium	Less than		2,400mg	2,400mg
Total Carbohydrate			300g	375g
Dietary Fiber			25g	30g

Calories per gram:
Fat 9 • Carbohydrate 4 • Protein 4

If you ate two cups of spinach, two cups of broccoli, one cup of green peas, one cup of blueberries, five carrots, an apple and a medium-sized potato, you'd deliver around 120 grams of carbohydrate through the FUD hatch. To deliver 300 grams per day, you almost have to eat refined sugars and starches. So that's what many of us did ... and many of us got fat as a result.

Back when I believed foods like meats and eggs are bad for us, I based my meals around rice, pasta, breads and cereals — just like the USDA told me to do. I also got fatter every year, in spite of lifting weights, jogging, and always trying to eat less. Well, no wonder. I was eating way more starch than I'm programmed to handle. My blood sugar was spiking after every meal, and Marty had to run the **Get Fatter!** program to bring it down.

When I finally figured out how my version of The Nautilus works, I cut all the refined starches from my diet. No more "healthy" cereals for breakfast. No more "healthy" whole-grain pasta for dinner. No more "healthy" fat-free pretzels for snacks. After making that change, I started losing weight without going hungry.

CHICKEN WITH CREAMED SPINACH, ROASTED SWEET POTATO, CARROT AND ONION

My diet still includes some starch, but it's just one part of a high-protein meal. And of course, the starches come from real foods like sweet potatoes and vegetables.

And that's the key: eating real food. Because as we'll see in the next chapter, industrial FUD doesn't just force Marty to run the **Get Fatter!** program after meals. It can also cause damage to The Nautilus that forces him to run the **Get Fatter!** program all the time.

8

HOW BAD FUD
DAMAGES THE FUEL SYSTEM

When you eat sugars and refined starches, you create an emergency that forces Marty to run the **Get Fatter!** program until your blood sugar returns to normal. That doesn't mean you can never eat pizza or potato chips or ice cream again. Yes, you'll store some fat, but if you don't damage the fuel system, Marty will eventually release the fat. It's okay to have a treat now and then — as long as it's now and then.

But if you eat food-like products too often, you can permanently damage the fuel system. When that happens, Marty ends up running the **Get Fatter!** program almost all the time. He isn't trying to make you feel frustrated or ashamed. He's simply reacting to a constant stream of emergencies that threaten the ship. Making you fat might cause problems for The Nautilus in the future, but Marty has to deal with what's happening RIGHT NOW.

Marty's non-stop emergencies begin with damage to the fuel system known as **insulin resistance**. Dr. Fishbones can explain.

When the fuel system is operating normally, insulin pushes glucose into the ship's cells, and the cells burn the glucose for energy. When cells become **insulin resistant**, they don't take delivery of the glucose. It's like they refuse to open the door. But Marty knows high blood sugar will damage The Nautilus, so he releases more insulin to kick open the door. If the cells become even more resistant, Marty can end up releasing insulin all day long.

INSULIN-RESISTANT CELLS DON'T RESPOND TO INSULIN

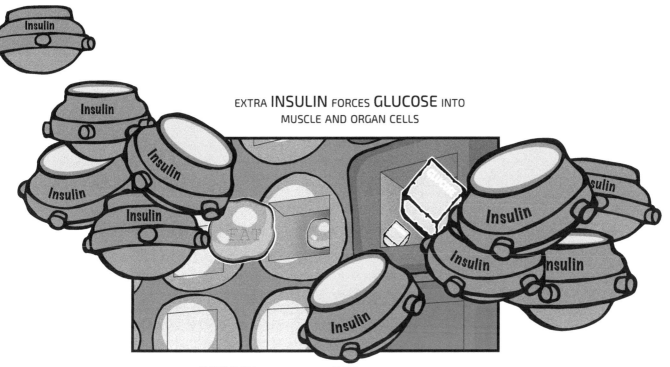

EXTRA **INSULIN** FORCES **GLUCOSE** INTO MUSCLE AND ORGAN CELLS

INSULIN ALSO PUSHES **FAT** INTO FAT CELLS

Unfortunately, it's another situation where solving one problem creates a new one. Extra insulin forces glucose into cells, but it also pushes fat into the fat cells and closes the door. So with all that insulin floating around the bloodstream, you keep storing fat. And to make matters worse, The Brain might conclude that you need to be *even fatter*. Mr. Spot will explain why.

As we've seen, Captain, fats are a crucial part of the fuel system. Therefore, The Brain monitors the fat supply. Fat cells communicate how much fat they contain by releasing a chemical messenger called leptin. The bigger the fat cells, the more leptin they release.

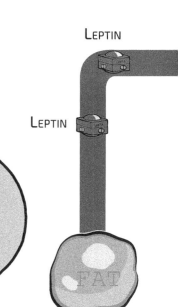

LEPTIN

LEPTIN

When The Brain receives sufficient leptin messages, it concludes that the fat supply is good. It then sends messages to Marty that it's okay to burn stored fat. Marty responds by shutting down the **Get Hungry!** program sooner and raising the metabolism.

THE BRAIN

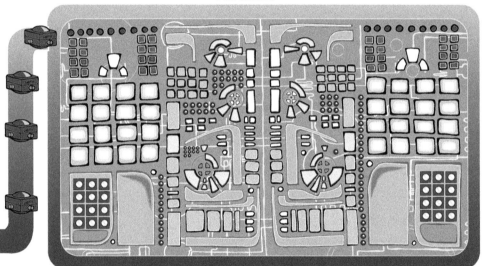

However, when The Brain doesn't receive sufficient leptin messages, it concludes that the fat supply is dangerously low. It then commands Marty to store more fat.

But Mr. Spot, you just said bigger fat cells release more leptin.
So shouldn't The Brain always know when The Nautilus is storing
too much fat?

Yes, Captain, it should know. But insulin resistance can
cause a breakdown in communications. When insulin is
high, it prevents leptin messages from reaching The Brain.
As a result, The Brain concludes that the fat supply is too
low and commands Marty to run the **Get Fatter!** program.

TO BRAIN

When the **Get Fatter!** program is running all the time, you're going to get fat, period. Remember the woman who suddenly became obese in her 30s? The tumor in her brain blocked the leptin messages from getting through. So her brain kept commanding Marty to run the **Get Fatter!** program. Every time she tried eating less, Marty responded by slowing down her metabolism. That's why she kept getting fatter while eating just 1500 calories per day.

Most people will never develop a brain tumor. But lots of people eat FUD that forces Marty to crank out more and more insulin. The high insulin blocks the leptin messages, so The Brain triggers the **Get Fatter!** program — even when The Nautilus is already storing too much fat. But getting fatter is only part of the problem. Dr. Fishbones will explain the bigger danger.

You have to remember why Marty releases all that insulin in the first place: to stop high blood sugar from damaging The Nautilus. But he can't keep it up forever. Insulin is produced in a small factory called the pancreas. If blood sugar keeps rising, the pancreas can't produce all the insulin Marty needs, so he can't keep the blood sugar under control anymore. That damages the ship in all kinds of ways.

THE PANCREAS PRODUCES INSULIN

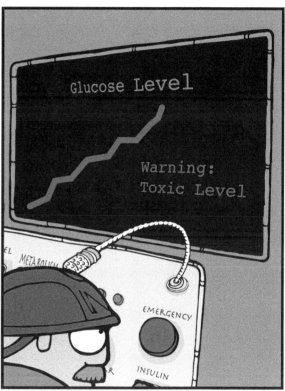

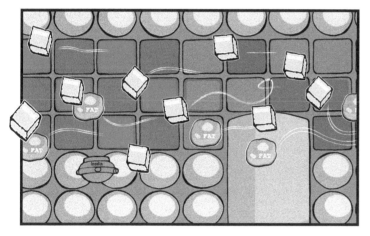

The condition Dr. Fishbones just described used to be called
adult onset diabetes because it mostly developed in adults.
These days it's called **type 2 diabetes** because teens and even
kids are developing it in record numbers. That never should have
happened. But it did ... because our modern diets include too
many food-like products The Nautilus wasn't designed to handle.

So which food-like products cause insulin resistance? Scientists are still working on that question. Different types of cells in The Nautilus may become insulin resistant for different reasons.

Unlike glucose, your body can't store fructose. The Liver can convert a bit of fructose to glucose, but not much. So it converts the rest of the fructose to fat. When The Liver becomes full of fat, it also becomes insulin resistant. So there's little doubt too much sugar causes one type of insulin resistance.

Sugar contains glucose and fructose

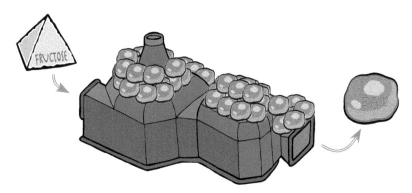

FRUCTOSE IS CONVERTED TO FAT IN THE LIVER

Some researchers believe we make our muscle cells insulin resistant by raising our blood sugar too high, too often, and for too long. When cells take in too much glucose, they become sticky and damaged. So they stop responding to insulin to avoid an overdose of glucose. Yes, the high blood sugar will damage other parts of the ship, but the cells are protecting themselves — because that's how they're programmed. As we've seen, refined carbohydrates raise glucose levels too high and for too long.

Some researchers also believe **inflammation** causes insulin resistance. If you scrape your knee, it swells up, turns red and feels warm. That's inflammation. If you have a fever, that's also inflammation. It's a counter-attack launched by a hugely important app we'll call **Sergeant Shockey**, the head of security.

YOUR **IMMUNE SYSTEM** KILLS GERMS WITH **HEAT**

Whenever there's a breech in The Nautilus, Shockey calls up her troops to fight off the alien invaders. Those troops use heat as one of their weapons. That's why you get a fever when you have an infection. The heat kills bacteria and viruses. When the invaders have been repelled, Shockey calls back the troops and the inflammation goes away.

If The Nautilus produces inflammation for a short time to fight an infection, that's good. But when inflammation is **chronic** — meaning it keeps going and going — that's not good. Heat is fine as a temporary weapon. But when it's used too often and for too long, it damages the ship's cells. When cells are damaged by inflammation, they often stop responding to insulin.

When we migrated to The Planet of the Preposterous Pyramid, we were told to eat industrial FUD. We were told that butter and lard cause heart disease, so we should switch to industrial vegetable oils. But those oils can spark inflammation all over the ship.

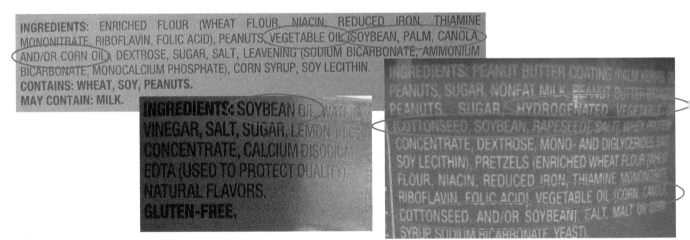

INDUSTRIAL OILS CAUSE **INFLAMMATION**

The natural oils that are squeezed directly from foods like olives are fine. In fact, they're good for you. But most "vegetable" oils sold today aren't squeezed from vegetables. They're chemically extracted from corn, soybeans or seeds. Perhaps Mr. Spot will tell us a little about the process.

Certainly, Captain. Industrial oils are extracted using a highly toxic chemical called **hexane**. The extracted oil is gray in color and has an odor your Earth children might call *Grody To The Max*. This wasn't a problem when the oils were originally developed, because they were mostly used for lubricating industrial machinery.

However, one of your fellow humans eventually had the bright idea of selling these oils as cheap replacements for butter and lard. So now the oils are bleached and de-odorized. Then artificial flavor and color are added before the oil is sold in an attractive package.

Well, at least these oils helped to prevent heart disease, right?

That is incorrect, Captain. Back when people in your country ate much more butter and lard, the rate of heart disease was quite low. It began rising during the decades when people switched to margarine and other industrial oils.

These oils were never meant to become part of The Nautilus. But as far as Marty knows, any fats you deliver through the FUD hatch are the natural fats that existed when the ship was designed. So he takes these industrial oils and does what he was programmed to do: he burns some for energy, and uses the rest for building materials.

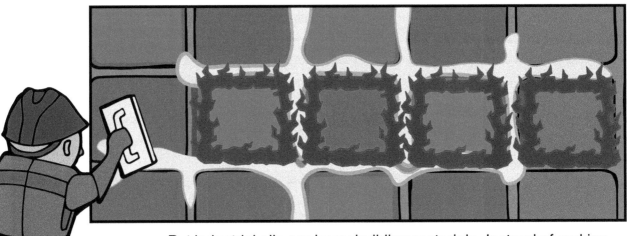

But industrial oils are lousy building materials. Instead of making our cells strong and flexible, they make cells brittle and weak. And when they're taken into our cells, industrial oils produce chemical reactions that cause inflammation.

Refined sugars can also cause inflammation. As we saw earlier, when you deliver a big load of fructose down the hatch, Marty sends some of it to The Liver to be stored as fat. This particular type of fat — called visceral fat — gets packed around your organs, not under your skin. The fat you can pinch under your skin is called subcutaneous fat.

Visceral fat is the "pot belly" fat, and it's the worst kind of fat to have. When too much fat is stored around the liver, it causes a condition called **fatty liver disease**. In previous generations, some adults developed a fatty liver by drinking too much alcohol. But now both adults and kids are developing fatty liver disease by consuming too much sugar. Dr. Fisbhones will explain why fatty liver disease is so dangerous.

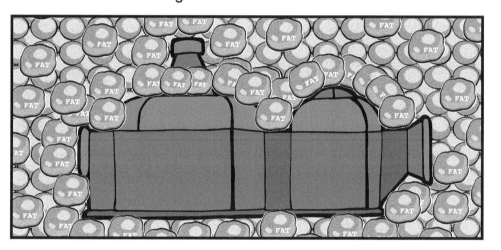

The Liver has many important jobs. It converts food into some of the tools and materials Marty needs. It also removes toxins from the bloodstream. When The Liver becomes full of fat, it doesn't do those jobs well. The fat also releases chemicals that cause inflammation. We know high insulin blocks leptin messages, Captain. But we believe inflammation blocks those messages as well. That means The Brain will command Marty to keep running the **Get Fatter!** program.

FAT-FREE CHOCOLATE MILK HAS 22 GRAMS OF SUGAR PER SERVING

Nutrition Facts

Serving Size: 1 CONTAINER (8oz)

Amount Per Serving

Calories 130	Fat Cal 0

	% Daily Value*
Total Fat 0g	0%
Sat Fat 0g	0%
Trans Fat 0g	
Cholest <5mg	2%
Sodium 180mg	8%
Potassium 460mg	13%
Total Carb 25g	8%
Fiber 0g	0%
Sugars 22g	
Protein 8g	16%

Vitamin A 10%	•	Vitamin C 0%
Calcium 30%	•	Iron 2%
Vitamin D 25%		

* Percent Daily Values are based on a 2,000 calorie diet

INGREDIENTS: FAT FREE MILK, SUGAR, COCOA PROCESSED WITH ALKALI, CORN STARCH, COCOA, SALT, CARRAGEENAN, GUAR GUM, NATURAL AND ARTIFICIAL FLAVOR, VITAMIN A PALMITATE AND VITAMIN D3 ADDED.

I hope you're beginning to understand why so many people these days are overweight. It's not because they're stupid or lack character. People didn't suddenly become lazy and weak-willed 35 years ago, when rates of obesity and diabetes began rising. Our health went downhill because we migrated to the wrong planets.

On The Planet of Industrial FUD, we began delivering refined flours and sugars through the FUD hatch. On The Planet of the Preposterous Pyramid, we were told to cut back on meats and eggs and deliver even more refined flours through the hatch. We were told to stop eating butter and lard and switch to industrial "vegetable" oils. The USDA ordered schools to stop serving whole milk with natural fats ... but kids are encouraged to drink fat-free chocolate milk that's full of refined sugar.

On these crazy planets, The Nautilus receives all the wrong chemical messages — and Marty ends up running the **Get Fatter!** program far too often, and for far too long.

I began this book by saying getting fat is about chemistry, not character. That's true. If you're fat, you didn't get that way by choosing to eat too much or exercise too little. You got fat because The Nautilus responded to chemical messages exactly as it was programmed to do.

But now that you understand how FUD triggers the **Get Fatter!** program, character does play a part. You have to decide to stop eating food-like products that send the wrong messages to Marty. You have to choose the real foods The Nautilus was designed to use for fuel and building materials.

As captain, that's your mission: to grab the controls and steer your ship back towards The Planet of Real Foods.

9

BAD FOOD MAKES BOY BOOBS

When I started getting fat around age 13, I was embarrassed by my fat belly. I was doubly embarrassed to have a fat belly with skinny arms and legs. But when I started growing "boy boobs" ... well, that was the biggest embarrassment of all. Trust me, it's no fun when classmates ask if you forgot your bra.

We all wore the same uniforms in gym class, so the gym teacher divided us into "shirts" and "skins" for team sports. I used to pray I'd end up on the shirts team. If I had to play without a shirt, I was too embarrassed about the boy boobs to focus on the game. That didn't improve my athletic performance.

Nearly 40 years too late, I learned that the boy boobs were caused by a bad diet. Just like with getting fat, it's all about those chemical messengers called **hormones**.

MY DAUGHTER WHEN SHE WAS LITTLE

When girls and boys are little, they don't look much different. Heck, you can hardly tell them apart. I remember a nice old guy in a mall pointing to my daughter and saying, "I bet he's going to be a slugger in the major leagues." I just smiled and thanked him. As a toddler with short hair, she did look like a boy.

But when boys and girls enter their teenage years, they become very different. (If you haven't noticed that by now, you may need glasses.) Girls become curvier. Boys grow thicker bones, thicker muscles and thicker vocal cords, which gives them a deeper voice.

Those changes happen when Marty and his construction crews receive instructions to build a bigger ship. The instructions arrive in the form of hormones, and they tell the crew what kind of ship The Nautilus should be. A bad diet can send the wrong instructions. Mr. Spot will explain.

All humans produce both male and female hormones. But as boys become adults, they produce more of a hormone called testosterone. This hormone instructs Marty's crews to build bigger bones, thicker muscles and a deeper voice. As girls become adults, they produce more of a hormone called estrogen. This hormone instructs the crews to build wider hips for carrying a baby and breasts for nursing children.

TESTOSTERONE   ESTROGEN

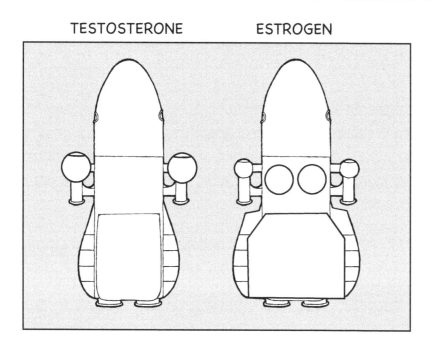

In other words, these hormones are like blueprints for a building. Without the right hormones, the crews don't know what to build. Or worse, they receive mixed-up instructions.

You don't eat hormones. The Nautilus has to build them from ingredients you deliver through the hatch. Many of those hormones are built largely from cholesterol. But on The Planet of the Preposterous Pyramid, we were told eating cholesterol will kill us. We were also told to cut way back on saturated fats. We'll have Mr. Spot explain how that affects the ship's hormones.

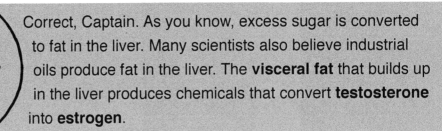

Several studies have demonstrated that when men switch from saturated fats to industrial vegetable oils, they produce less testosterone. That's not a good result, Captain.

Definitely not. On The Planet of Industrial FUD, people also eat a lot more sugar and refined grains. Those foods cause high blood sugar. When blood sugar is high, The Nautilus produces less testerosterone. So it's little wonder that men today produce less testosterone than men in previous generations.

And to make matters worse, a bad diet can alter testosterone even after it's built. Isn't that right, Mr. Spot?

Correct, Captain. As you know, excess sugar is converted to fat in the liver. Many scientists also believe industrial oils produce fat in the liver. The **visceral fat** that builds up in the liver produces chemicals that convert **testosterone** into **estrogen**.

Yup, you heard Mr. Spot correctly. A bad diet creates belly fat that can turn your "man" hormones into "woman" hormones. When that happens, Marty's crews receive instructions to build female parts. So you end up with boy boobs.

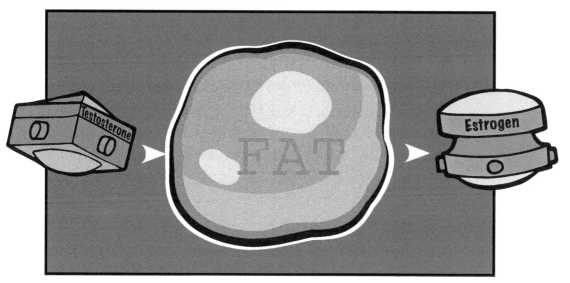

VISCERAL FAT IN THE LIVER PRODUCES CHEMICALS THAT CONVERT TESTOSTERONE INTO ESTROGEN

And boy boobs are just part of the problem. Most boys become a LOT stronger as teenagers because testosterone instructs Marty's crew to build bigger muscles. The more testosterone, the bigger and stronger the muscles. Testosterone also helps men burn fat.

If only I'd known that when I was your age. Thanks to all the breads and sugary cereals in my diet, I grew a big belly around age 13. At exactly the time I should have been building strong muscles, my building crews were seeing too much estrogen and not enough testosterone. So they built what the hormones told them to build. I ended up with wider hips and smaller muscles than I should have. And the boy boobs.

The wrong hormones can send the wrong instructions at any time in a man's life, which is why some men don't develop "man boobs" until they're older. But trust me, you really, really, really don't want it to happen when Marty's crews are expanding your ship from a boy into a man. During your teenage years, your body will grow more rapidly than it ever will again. It's crucial that the construction crews receive the right instructions.

If you're already getting fat and developing boy boobs, don't panic. It's not too late to stop converting testosterone into estrogen. But to do that, you need to stop eating FUD that sends the wrong messages — as soon as possible.

10

THOSE "HEALTHY WHOLE GRAINS" ARE NOT HEALTH FOOD

Take another look at this poster from the 1940s. These were the "protective" foods people were told to eat every day: meat, eggs, milk, butter, fruit, vegetables and a potato.

Notice what isn't in this poster? That's right: there's no bread, no cereal, no pasta. In other words, no grains. Hardly anyone back then thought you had to eat grains to be healthy. In fact, when I was in high school, our health teacher (who was also the wrestling coach) told us to stop eating sugar and grains if we wanted to lose weight. Well, heck, what did he know? All he did was help hundreds of athletes get down to their competition weight.

That was in the 1970s. In the early 1990s, the USDA introduced the Food Pyramid, which told us to do exactly the opposite. Now we were supposed to eat more grains than anything else — between six and 11 servings per day. Welcome to The Planet of the Preposterous Pyramid.

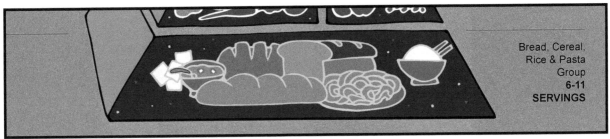

Bread, Cereal, Rice & Pasta Group 6-11 SERVINGS

THE **FOOD PYRAMID** TOLD US TO EAT **6-11** SERVINGS OF **GRAINS** PER DAY

If you're interested in health, you've probably seen a steady stream of media articles declaring the wonders of whole grains. **Whole grains prevent diabetes! Whole grains prevent weight gain! Whole grains prevent heart disease!** So how can grains possibly be bad for you?

To understand what those studies actually show, let's return to Mr. Spot's universe and have him explain a bit more about science.

The important concept to grasp, Captain, is that *less bad* isn't the same as *good*. Suppose we compare the health of people who smoke filtered or unfiltered cigarettes. Filters remove some of the toxins in smoke. So people who smoke filtered cigarettes will have lower rates of cancer. But that doesn't mean filtered cigarettes prevent cancer. It only means they are less likely to *cause* cancer than unfiltered cigarettes.

The same logic applies to studies of whole grains. Researchers compare people who eat whole grains to people who eat white flour. Whole grains don't spike blood sugar as quickly as white flour, so they are less likely to cause health problems. But that doesn't mean whole grains are good. It means they're less bad.

Exactly. Because the truth is that many "whole grain" breads and cereals spike your blood sugar faster than if you ate sugar directly from the bowl.

When I tell people wheat isn't good for them, they sometimes reply, "How can that be? People have been eating wheat forever! They talk about breaking bread in the Bible!"

But we haven't been eating wheat forever. For more than 99 percent of the time after it was created, The Nautilus lived on The Planet of Real Foods. We didn't start eating wheat until we migrated to The Planet of FUD Farms. It's just silly to believe that the health of The Nautilus depends on food that didn't exist when it was designed and programmed.

Before we migrated to The Planet of Industrial FUD, people ground wheat berries into flour and made their own bread. That bread was high in fiber, and most of the carbohydrates were locked inside cells. I've seen heated debates about whether this old-fashioned bread was good, bad, or just okay. Personally, I don't believe bread was ever a good food. But it doesn't matter, because that's not the bread people eat today.

Today, almost all FUD made from wheat has been refined. It's processed on machines that remove the fibers and smash the cells. Even the "whole wheat" bread sold today is made from refined flour with a bit of fiber sprinkled back in. That's why it spikes your blood sugar.

But modern wheat can also cause damage to The Nautilus that has nothing to do with blood sugar. That's because modern wheat can trick your body into attacking itself.

As we saw earlier, when FUD comes down the hatch, Chef Chop-Chop slices up the nutrients so they can slip through security filters that protect the ship. Those filters are called tight junctions. But modern wheat (and other grains) can ruin those filters. Dr. Fishbones will explain what happens.

Most grains contain a sticky substance called gluten. The **gluten** contains a protein called gliadin. The **gliadin** in modern wheat can bang through the **tight junctions** in the digestive system. That's bad enough, but it gets worse. Once those security filters are damaged, FUD particles that shouldn't be in the bloodstream can slip through. Doctors call this condition leaky gut syndrome.

GLIADIN

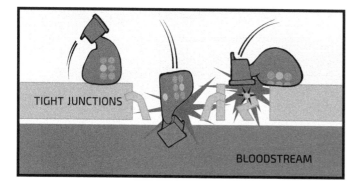

TIGHT JUNCTIONS

BLOODSTREAM

GLIADIN BANGS THROUGH TIGHT JUNCTIONS, ALLOWING FOREIGN PARTICLES INTO BLOODSTREAM

When The Nautilus sees particles in the bloodstream that shouldn't be there, it launches an attack against the alien invaders. Alarms start ringing, and Sergeant Shockey calls up the troops. Those troops use heat as one of their weapons, which causes inflammation. So once you develop a leaky gut, you may have inflammation all the time.

All that heat damages the ship, but that's only part of the problem. Before Sergeant Shockey sends the troops into action, she has to tell them what the invaders look like. Most alien invaders wear a coat made of protein. So Shockey scouts the FUD particles that have invaded the bloodstream, identifies the proteins, and informs the troops.

Unfortunately, the proteins worn by the invading FUD particles can look very much like the proteins in your own tissues. So when Shockey's troops go on the attack, they end up attacking structures within The Nautilus itself. It's a case of mistaken identity.

WAY TO GO, TROOPS!

AAGGGHHH!

SHOCKEY'S TROOPS MISTAKENLY ATTACK OUR OWN TISSUES

When the body attacks itself, it's called an **autoimmune disease**. Exactly where your body attacks itself depends on your version of The Nautilus. An autoimmune attack can cause arthritis, asthma, skin rashes, constant belly aches, and dozens of other ailments.

Once gliadin invades the bloodstream, it can travel to The Brain and cause malfunctions there — like a virus that infects a computer and messes with the code. Gliadin may be partly what triggers mental problems like Attention Deficit Disorder and Schizophrenia.

Can we say that for sure? No, because scientists aren't going to conduct diet experiments that turn people into schizophrenics. But as Mr. Spot will explain, scientists can tell when gliadin was at the scene of an attack.

Sergeant Shockey calls up different types of soldiers to fight different types of invaders. These soldiers are known as **antibodies**. People who suffer from Attention Deficit Disorder and Schizophrenia often have a high level of **gliadin antibodies** in their bloodstreams. So logically, we know Sergeant Shockey has been responding to an invasion of gliadin.

GLIADIN ANTIBODIES

I gave up wheat after realizing it spikes my blood sugar. I figured I'd lose weight more easily, and I did. But then a funny thing happened: all kinds of annoying health problems went away.

I used to have arthritis in my left shoulder. I had a type of skin rash called **psoriasis** on the back of my head. I had frequent belly aches and sinus infections. I often had backaches or pains in my legs that kept me awake at night. I had a mild case of asthma.

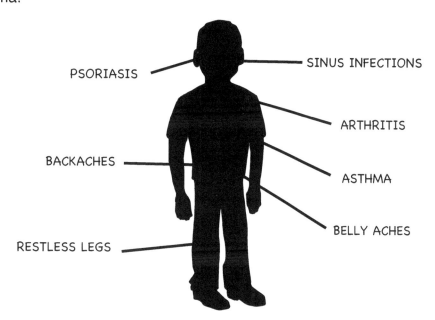

When I gave up wheat, every single one of those ailments went away — and they've never come back. I was delighted, but also surprised. These seemed like totally separate health problems. How could they all be related to eating wheat?

Now I know. It was the gliadin in those "healthy" whole-grain cereals and breads I was eating. Those foods were damaging my security filters and causing a leaky gut.

According to one study, almost everyone who consumes gliadin ends up with at least some of it in the bloodstream. Some people are lucky and don't feel the effects. The ones who aren't so lucky end up with inflammation and perhaps an autoimmune disease ... or two, or three. Most doctors never trace the diseases back to the gliadin. They just prescribe drugs to treat the effects.

Sometimes the drugs are necessary. Sometimes they're life-savers. But it's way, way better to avoid developing those diseases in the first place.

You avoid those diseases by avoiding FUD The Nautilus was never designed to handle. Modern wheat is one of those foods.

11

FOOD SETS THE MOOD

One of the nicest letters I've ever received was from a mom. After watching my film *Fat Head*, she changed her family's diet because she and her husband wanted to lose weight. They did. They were happy about that ... but far happier to see how the new diet affected their teenage son.

For years, their son struggled in school because he couldn't concentrate. He had a hot temper and flew into rages over little annoyances.

But after leaving The Planet of Industrial FUD, he became a different person. He likes to read now and does well in school. He's a happy, even-tempered young guy. His mother was simply amazed by the change. She thanked me for changing his life.

I didn't change his life. Returning to The Planet of Real Food changed his life.

It's great to lose weight and become stronger. It's great to be free of nagging ailments like arthritis and skin rashes. But even if you never develop those ailments, it's hard to enjoy life if you constantly feel cranky or depressed.

An awful lot of adults these days are in therapy because they're unhappy. Some of them probably need therapy. But as a therapist friend of mine likes to say, all the therapy in the world won't undo the effects of a bad diet. To a large degree, food sets the mood ... because what you eat has a huge effect on The Brain.

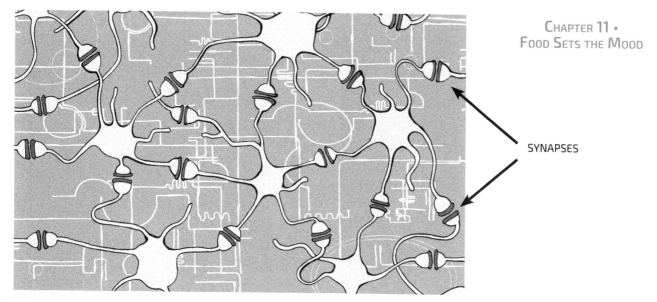

SYNAPSES

The Brain is like any other computer: to work efficiently and well, it needs quality parts and a steady supply of energy.

As we saw earlier, The Brain is made mostly from fat. If you want a quality brain, you need quality fats — the natural fats that existed when The Nautilus was designed, not industrial oils. That means real butter and other animal fats. It means oils that were squeezed directly from real foods like olives and coconuts.

The Brain receives messages through transmitters called synapses. Those synapses are made largely from **cholesterol**. Take away the cholesterol, and The Brain doesn't receive and process messages like it should. So it shouldn't surprise us that people with very low cholesterol often have mental problems, as Mr. Spot will explain.

Indeed, Captain. A number of studies show that people with very low cholesterol are more likely to become depressed. They're more likely to be arrested for violent crimes. They're more likely to harm themselves.

So to keep The Brain humming along efficiently, you have to keep delivering natural fats and cholesterol through the hatch. Those are the quality parts it needs.

I learned that the hard way. When I first migrated to The Planet of the Preposterous Pyramid, I went on very low-fat diets. But each time I tried cutting all the cholesterol and most of the fat from my diet, I ended up feeling depressed. Now that I'm a "fat head" (my term for someone who eats a lot of natural fats), I'm never depressed.

But even a well-built brain needs a steady supply of fuel. The wrong kind of FUD can mess up the fuel supply. Here's an example:

Some years ago, I had an all-day meeting with another programmer to plan a complicated software system. When lunch time came around, I had a salad with chicken. He had a sandwich on white bread, a bag of chips and a soda. Two hours later, I was still alert and ready to work. But he plopped down in his chair and said, "Sorry, man, we'll have to pick this up tomorrow. I can't think anymore. My brain's fried."

FUD THAT MESSES UP
THE FUEL SYSTEM

His brain wasn't fried. It was low on fuel. Why? By this point, you can probably guess. All those refined carbohydrates in his lunch spiked his blood sugar. Marty responded to the emergency by flooding the bloodstream with insulin. As a result, my fellow programmer ended up with low blood sugar. The Brain bogged down and he couldn't focus on a complicated subject anymore.

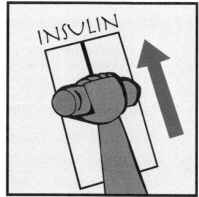

Fortunately, he didn't lose his temper and yell at me or anything. When their blood sugar drops below normal, people often become ridiculously angry. Once again, it's all about how Marty is programmed to protect the ship.

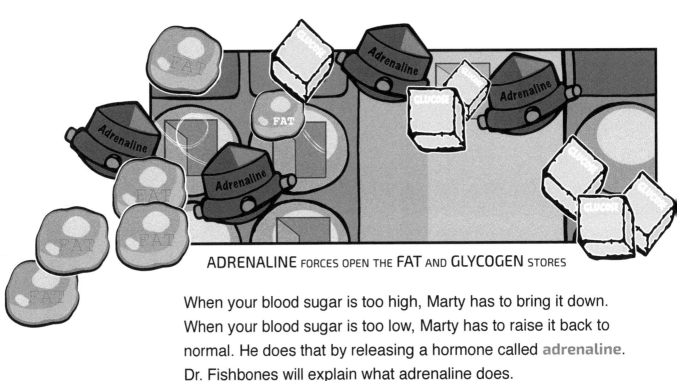

ADRENALINE FORCES OPEN THE FAT AND GLYCOGEN STORES

When your blood sugar is too high, Marty has to bring it down. When your blood sugar is too low, Marty has to raise it back to normal. He does that by releasing a hormone called adrenaline. Dr. Fishbones will explain what adrenaline does.

We doctors call **adrenaline** the "fight or flight" hormone. There's always some adrenaline in your bloodstream, because it keeps The Heart beating. But in an emergency, Marty releases a burst of adrenaline to force open the fat stores and the glycogen stores. That way the ship has the energy to engage in battle or fly away in a hurry.

Marty will also release adrenaline to raise the blood sugar when it's too low. That's exactly what happened in one study, Captain. Kids were given a breakfast of instant oatmeal with sugar. Their blood sugar went too high, then it went too low. Then their bodies released adrenaline to raise their blood sugar back to normal.

So ... what kind of mood are you in when your body is preparing for a fight? Probably not in the mood to read a book. Or focus on math homework. Or act like a nice person. But you almost certainly feel angry — because being angry helps you fight.

Even if you don't throw temper-tantrums, a bad diet can make you feel lazy. Remember the mom in the grocery store? She was going to make her son play outdoors because he was getting fat. That's what most people believe: kids get lazy, and then they get fat from sitting around. That's why there are national campaigns telling kids to go out and play.

I hope kids do go out and play. Being active is good for you. But the research on this subject is crystal clear. Kids don't get fat because they stop moving as much.

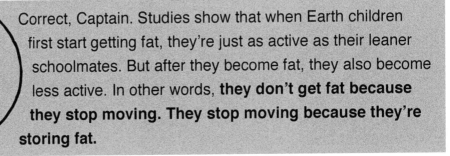

Correct, Captain. Studies show that when Earth children first start getting fat, they're just as active as their leaner schoolmates. But after they become fat, they also become less active. In other words, **they don't get fat because they stop moving. They stop moving because they're storing fat.**

If you think about how the fuel system works, it makes perfect sense. We get fat when Marty starts running the **Get Fatter!** program too often and for too long. With more fuel being stored, there's not enough left for The Nautilus to constantly fly around. So Marty sends out chemical messages that tell you to slow down. That's when other people decide you're just being lazy.

When I was a skinny kid, I wasn't very athletic. But I was certainly active. I was always running around outside with my friends. Nobody had to tell us **Let's Move!** or **Play 60!** If anything, our moms had to yell at us to come inside for dinner.

When I started getting fat, that all changed. Running around outside wasn't so appealing anymore. I still played outside, but nowhere near as often.

By the time I was in my 30s, I felt tired way too often. I exercised at a gym now and then, and I even took up jogging to try to lose weight. But I still got a little fatter each year, and I never enjoyed the hard work. It was just something I made myself do, like it or not.

I'm 58 now, and my energy level is way higher than it was 20 years ago. As a programmer and writer, I work at a desk. But I get up and move around several times per day — because I feel like moving. I lift weights at a gym every week, and I look forward to it — really and truly. On weekends, I'm always looking for something physical to do outside. I play disc golf on a course I built on my own land.
I spend hours knocking down weeds, or mowing the back pastures, or cutting up wood, or building fences, or building a bridge across the creek.

Nobody has to tell me to go out and exercise. I move because I want to move. My brain is humming along, my body is full of energy, and I'm almost always in a good mood.
That isn't about character. It's about chemistry. I didn't suddenly develop more discipline in my 50s. I changed my chemistry by changing the kind of FUD I deliver through the hatch. You can do the same.

12

GOOD SLEEP IS ALMOST AS IMPORTANT AS GOOD FOOD

For the most part, we've been looking at why you need a good diet. But before we go on, I want to mention something else you need to be happy and healthy: good sleep — and lots of it.

As a busy guy with a lot of interests, I understand the temptation to burn the candle at both ends. After all, when we're sleeping, there are good TV shows on that we're not watching. There are video games that we're not playing. There are likes and dislikes on social media that we're not seeing.

Those super-important distractions can wait. If you want The Nautilus to perform at a high level, they have to wait.

The Nautilus is a hugely complicated machine that needs daily rebuilding and repairs. Marty and his crews have to do some of those repair jobs when the ship is powered down. If you don't keep the ship powered down long enough, they can't finish the work. That means The Nautilus will start to break down.

ALL RIGHT, LOOKS LIKE WE HAVE TO QUIT FOR THE DAY.

The Brain has to power down for long periods as well, or it will malfunction. I recently read a book by a psychiatrist who works with kids. One of his patients was a high-school girl who was diagnosed with attention-deficit disorder. She couldn't focus, her grades were slipping, and she was overly emotional. The family doctor put her on drugs for ADD.

But she didn't have attention-deficit disorder. She had a sleep-deficit disorder. She had been secretly staying up half the night to check her social media pages. She was only sleeping a few hours each night. That isn't enough for anyone, and certainly not enough for a growing girl. When she started sleeping at least eight hours each night, the "attention-deficit disorder" went away.

Going short on sleep can also make you fatter. As The Nautilus begins to break down, other crew members send distress messages to Marty. Those messages arrive in the form of a hormone called **cortisol**. Like adrenaline, we need some cortisol to function. But also like adrenaline, cortisol raises blood sugar. So when there's too much cortisol in the bloodstream, your blood sugar goes too high. Marty responds by releasing extra insulin and running the **Get Fatter!** program.

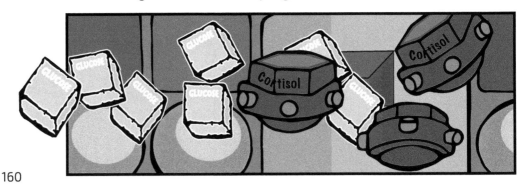

GOING SHORT ON SLEEP CAN MAKE YOU FATTER

If you're a guy, going short on sleep can also prevent you from building the muscles you want. Mr. Spot will explain why:

As we've seen, Captain, the hormone **testosterone** instructs the ship's crew to build stronger muscles. Human males produce most of their testosterone while sleeping. So logically, the less sleep, the less testosterone. And in fact, that's what a recent study demonstrated. Men who slept four hours per night produced just half as much testosterone as men who slept eight hours per night.

And remember, testosterone doesn't just build muscle. It also helps keep you lean. When your testosterone level drops, Marty is more likely to convert extra calories into fat instead of muscle.

If you don't want to believe an old guy like me, perhaps this will convince you: if you're an NFL football fan, you're familiar with a player for the Houston Texans named J.J. Watt — the defensive end who terrorizes opposing quarterbacks. The guy is amazingly fast and amazingly strong.

During a TV show about the team's training camp, Watt gave some advice to a rookie: if you want to be as strong as you can be, you need to sleep at least nine hours per night.

That's great advice for an NFL rookie — and for any other version of The Nautilus.

13

To Stay Healthy
You Need to Feed
Trillions of Your Closest Friends

Here's one of the great things about science: no matter how much we learn, there's always more to know. For years, it seemed as if scientists knew almost everything about The Nautilus. They could tell us how FUD is digested. They could tell us how fats, proteins and carbohydrates are used inside the ship. They could explain how nutrients are removed from FUD before the leftovers travel to the garbage chute — a final section of the digestive system called the **colon**.

The garbage chute didn't get much attention. Most people only thought about it when it became clogged. Then some scientists decided to give that garbage chute a closer look. Boy, were they in for a surprise.

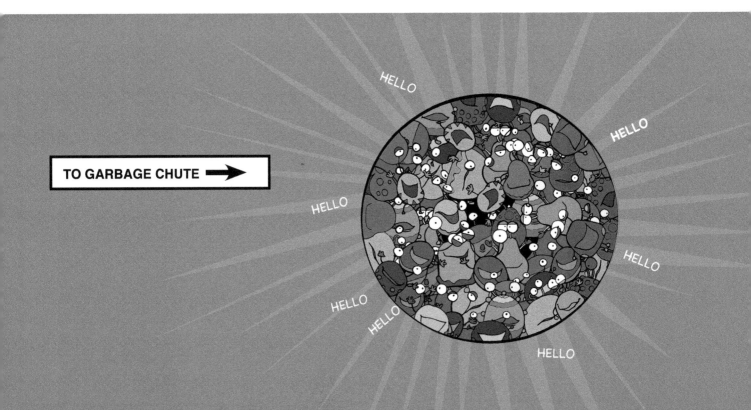

TO GARBAGE CHUTE ➡

Yup, it turns out there are trillions of additional crew members living there. They've been living there ever since The Nautilus was designed. We just didn't have the technology to notice them, because they're incredibly small. They're also incredibly important.

This is a new area of science, so there's a lot scientists still don't know about these crew members. But there's plenty they do know, as Mr. Spot will explain.

The part of the ship you're referring to is known as the gut microbiome, Captain. The crew members who live there are known as gut bacteria, or simply gut bugs. They're quite fascinating. We've learned that when alien bacteria invade the digestive system, gut bugs provide troops for Sergeant Shockey to use in a counter-attack. Research demonstrates that they also send frequent chemical messages to The Brain. That's probably why humans speak of having a "gut feeling" about something.

ALIEN BACTERIA

GOOD GUT BUGS

GOOD GUT BUGS HELP YOUR IMMUNE SYSTEM

Furthermore, research shows that gut bugs send messages to Marty, and that he responds to those messages. Gut bugs, for example, can trigger the **Get Fatter!** program. Or they can send Marty a message that it's okay to burn stored fat.

You mean these incredibly tiny gut bugs can make us fatter or thinner?

Indeed, Captain. If scientists transplant gut bugs from a fat mouse to a skinny mouse, the skinny mouse becomes fat. If they transplant gut bugs from a skinny mouse to a fat mouse, the fat mouse becomes thinner. If they transplant gut bugs from a mouse with diabetes to a healthy mouse, the healthy mouse develops diabetes.

If some gut bugs make us healthier and others make us sicker, then obviously there are good bugs and bad bugs living in the chute. They're kind of like opposing armies who both want to take over the entire territory. To stay healthy, you need to help the good bugs win. At this point, it probably won't surprise you if I say the FUD you deliver through the hatch is what makes the difference.

As scientists are now learning, The Nautilus apparently struck a deal with the gut bugs at the very beginning: they live in the chute and help keep the ship healthy. In return, they get to eat our leftovers.

Remember all the fibers and other bits of FUD that Chef Chop-Chop sends on down the chute? We don't use that stuff for energy or building materials, so most scientists figured it's just garbage. We poop it out, so we probably never needed it in the first place — or so we thought.

But it turns out the "garbage" is what feeds our trillions of friends living in the chute. At least we hope we're feeding our friends. When we feed the good bugs, they reproduce faster and take over the chute. But if we feed the bad bugs, they reproduce faster and take over the chute.

On The Planet of Real Foods, humans gathered plants full of natural fibers. The good bugs love to eat fibers from foods like peas, broccoli, lentils, spinach, artichokes, onions, berries, carrots and nuts. On The Planet of Real Foods, humans also gathered root vegetables and tubers. Those plants contain a type of starch called resistant starch. It's called **resistant** because we don't break it down and use it for fuel — but the good gut bugs do.

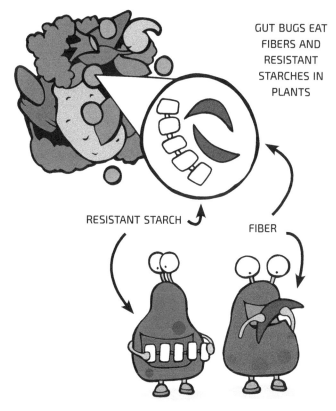

GUT BUGS EAT FIBERS AND RESISTANT STARCHES IN PLANTS

RESISTANT STARCH

FIBER

When the good gut bugs eat these fibers and resistant starches, they produce a special type of fat. This fat can provide The Nautilus with a bit of extra fuel, but that's a small benefit. Dr. Fishbones will explain the big benefits.

The special fat is called butyrate, Captain. It helps to keep the entire digestive system healthy. It reduces inflammation. It protects against the leaky-gut problem we saw earlier. It helps Marty keep the blood sugar under control. It triggers chemical messages that tell Marty to shut down the **Get Hungry!** program. In other words, it helps The Nautilus repair some of the damage caused by a bad diet. I could go on and on about—

Thank you, Doctor, I'm sure you could. But I believe it's important to mention that we also need to prevent the bad bugs from reproducing. Research shows that refined carbohydrates and industrial oils create an environment that allows the bad bugs to flourish in the chute.

I was getting to that, Spot! Feed the good bugs, don't feed the bad bugs. That's what I wanted to say.

But you can't feed the good bugs if they're not on board the ship. Back when The Nautilus was created, people gathered plants, washed them a bit, then ate them. Those plants were covered with good bugs that ended up in the chute. Today we'd consider those foods too dirty. So we wash and wash and wash the food. That helps prevent food poisoning, which is good. But all that washing also removes many of the good bugs.

We also take antibiotics when we're sick with the flu or other infections. Don't get me wrong; antibiotics have saved millions of lives by killing deadly bacteria that invaded the ship. But antibiotics also kill off the good gut bugs living in the chute.

So to help the good bugs win, we need to bring in reinforcements. We can do that by taking probiotics — pills that contain billions of good gut bugs. But we can also deliver good bugs through the hatch by eating foods that have been **fermented**.

A food becomes **fermented** when good bugs have already eaten part of it and started reproducing. People throughout history have made and eaten fermented foods, which usually have a tangy taste. In central Europe, they ate sauerkraut. In northern Europe, they ate pickled fish. In Asia, they ate a mix of fermented vegetables called kimchi. In both Europe and Asia, people fermented milk to make yogurt.

These people probably knew nothing about gut bugs. But they knew eating fermented foods kept them healthy. If you've been having trouble digesting FUD, or if you're struggling with your weight, eating fermented foods is something you ought to try.

And after you deliver the good bugs through the hatch, feed them by eating real foods that contain fibers and resistant starch. You need those good guys to take over the chute.

FERMENTATION HELPS TO PRESERVE FOOD

FERMENTED FOODS REPLENISH YOUR GUT MICROBIOME
AND HELP YOU STAY HEALTHY

14

My Whole Life
Could Have Been Different

No matter what I ate as a kid, I was never going to be a great athlete ... or even just a guy with big, popping muscles. To explain why, we'll have Dr. Fishbones talk briefly about body types.

ECTOMORPH

ENDOMORPH

MESOMORPH

There are three basic body types for humans, Captain. Ectomorphs have thin bones and tend to be skinny all over. Endomorphs have thick bones and also tend to be thick through the middle. They gain weight more easily than other people. The lucky people are mesomorphs. They're narrow in the waist, but tend to grow big muscles. That's because more of their muscles are made from what we call **fast-twitch muscle fibers**. Those are the fibers that grow bigger when you exercise. They're also the fibers that give people athletic quickness.

Must be great for the mesomorphs. Here's how an article in *Men's Fitness* magazine described them:

> *Mesomorphs look well built without setting foot in a gym, and pack on muscle the instant they pick up a dumbbell.*

I knew guys like that. I wanted to be a guy like that. But I'm not a mesomorph. Most of us are a mix of the three body types, and I'm mostly an ectomorph. I have the thin bones ... but I also tend to get thick through the middle.

So I was never going to be a great athlete. I was never going to be the star quarterback and win the hearts of all the pretty cheerleaders. I didn't inherit the traits to make that possible.

But here's what I finally learned so many years later: I didn't have to be the slowest, weakest guy in class, either. I didn't have to be a fat kid with skinny arms and legs. I didn't have to end up with boy boobs. I didn't inherit that body. I told Marty to build that body by eating the wrong FUD and sending the wrong messages.

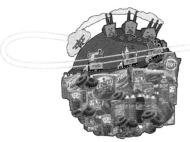

THE PLANET OF
INDUSTRIAL FUD

I grew up on The Planet of Industrial FUD. As a young adult, I migrated to The Planet of The Preposterous Pyramid, along with millions of other people. Throughout much of my life, I ate cereal for breakfast — sugary cereal as a kid, and "healthy" cereals like Grape-Nuts as an adult. As a kid, I ate sandwiches on white bread. As an adult, I spread margarine made from industrial oils on my whole-wheat toast. I drank big glasses of orange juice. I ate pasta for dinner. It seemed everyone was warning that saturated fat would kill us, so I ate fat-free pretzels for snacks. I was sure I was making smart choices.

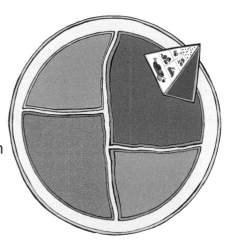

THE PLANET OF THE
PREPOSTEROUS PYRAMID

Now that you've learned how The Nautilus works, think about the messages that diet was sending to Marty.

The FUD was low in protein, micronutrients and quality fats, so Marty kept running the **Get Hungry!** program even after I'd eaten. All those refined carbohydrates raised my blood sugar too high, too often, and for too long. Marty had to respond to the blood-sugar emergencies by running the **Get Fatter!** program.

Often he had to dump so much insulin into my bloodstream, I ended up with low blood sugar. Then I felt tired and depressed ... or ridiculously angry as the adrenaline kicked in.

The sugars created fat in my liver, which produced inflammation. The inflammation and high blood sugar caused insulin resistance, which forced Marty to pump out more insulin. The high insulin prevented The Brain from seeing the leptin messages from my fat cells, so The Brain concluded I was running low on fat and ordered Marty to run the **Get Fatter!** program.

The fat in my liver also converted some of my testosterone into estrogen. That told the construction crews to build boy boobs — and didn't tell them to build bigger, stronger muscles.

The gliadin in all the wheat I was eating poked holes in the security filters in my digestive system. That allowed foreign particles into my bloodstream, which forced Sergeant Shockey to go on the attack against the invaders.

But some of those invaders were wearing protein coats that looked like the proteins in my own tissues. So Shockey's troops attacked my own tissues and I ended up with arthritis, asthma, skin rashes, twitchy legs, and frequent belly aches.

Not a pretty picture, is it? But the same thing is happening to millions of people, including kids. And when those people get fatter and sicker, the overlords on The Planet of the Preposterous Pyramid tell them it's their own fault.

They cite the Piggy Bank Theory and tell people to just eat less and exercise more ... oh, and they should also cut *even more* natural fat from their diets and eat *even more* processed grain. That's like trying to cure a headache by hitting yourself in the head with a hammer. You can't fix The Nautilus by delivering more FUD it wasn't programmed to handle.

Now let's think about what happened when I migrated back to The Planet of Real Foods. On this planet, I eat meat, eggs, fish, nuts, vegetables, tubers and whole fruits. All the fats are natural fats, like butter, cream, olive oil and coconut oil.

These real foods are higher in protein, micronutrients and quality fats. Marty gets what he needs and shuts down the **Get Hungry!** program sooner.

The fibers and the cells in the unprocessed plant foods force Chef Chop-Chop to process the glucose a little at a time, so Marty doesn't have to run the **Get Fatter!** program to deal with an emergency.

My blood sugar stays nice and steady, so The Brain has the fuel it needs and I'm able to concentrate for long hours. The Brain also gets the fats and cholesterol it needs, so I'm in a good mood almost all the time.

My good gut bugs are happy because I feed them well. I don't have to count calories because my appetite is controlled naturally — exactly how The Nautilus was designed to work.

If I'd understood all this when I was your age, I know my life would have been different. I would have saved myself a lot of frustration and embarrassment. I would have been leaner, stronger, and more energetic. I would have enjoyed playing outdoors more. I would have gone to the beach and taken off my shirt without feeling embarrassed. I would have asked out the pretty girls I liked, instead of telling myself they wouldn't be interested in a guy with skinny arms and a fat belly.

I'm grateful that I finally figured it out as I approached age 50. As the saying goes, better late than never. But you don't have to make that choice. For you, the choice is sooner rather than later. You just have to decide it's time to steer your ship back towards The Planet of Real Foods.

15

STUFF I WISH I KNEW WHEN I WAS YOUR AGE:

IT'S PERFECTLY GOOD TO BE GOOD INSTEAD OF PERFECT

If you read a lot about diet and health (as I do), you'll come across people who believe your diet has to be perfect or you'll get sick and die. Every ounce of meat has to come from animals raised in grassy pastures. You can only eat fruit that traveled less than 100 miles. All your vegetables have to be raised by a barefoot hippie farmer who doesn't use pesticides and only takes a bath on Saturday night. And so forth.

Some of those perfectly pure foods do provide more nutrients. But if you try to live on The Planet of the Perfectly Pure Diet, you might just go a little bonkers — and it will cost your parents a lot of money. But you don't need a perfectly pure diet to become leaner and healthier. You just need a good diet. Or as I like to say, **it's perfectly good to be good instead of perfect**.

The first and most important step on the journey back to good health is to stop damaging The Nautilus. You can do that by following three simple rules:

- **Don't eat refined sugar**
- **Don't eat refined grains**
- **Don't eat industrial "vegetable" oils**

Once you've taken that step, it's time to set a course back to The Planet of Real Foods. If you haven't spent much time there, you may wonder how you'll recognize the place. Actually, it's easy.

On The Planet of Real Foods, the FUD looks like something that could exist in Nature. It looks like this:

FUD that wouldn't exist without industrial processing isn't real food. There are no Pop-Tart plants in Nature. There are no cereal bushes, no bread stalks, no trees with big boxes of apple juice hanging from the branches, no pasta flowers, and no bottles of industrial "vegetable" oils made from corn, cotton seeds, soybeans, or canola seeds. Those are the food-like products the Nautilus was never designed to handle.

Again, you don't have to be perfect. When my daughters go to birthday parties, it's fine with their mother and me if they eat the chips, pizza, cake and ice cream. When we go out for dinner, they can split a dessert if they want one. It's okay to visit The Planet of Industrial FUD now and then. But if you're fat and want to lose weight, you can't live there. If you're not fat but want to be stronger and healthier, you can't live there.

It's perfectly good for your body to be good instead of perfect as well. I'm sure we'd all love to look like star athletes or models. But most of us can't. We inherit many of our traits, and we can't trade them in for a new set, just like we can't change how The Nautilus is programmed.

So when you begin your journey to better health, be realistic about the final destination. Rate your performance as captain on how well you stay on course, not on whether you reach a particular size or shape.

If you're struggling with your weight, I want you to know I've been where you are. I felt the emotional sting of the insults from leaner, stronger guys. I felt my face turn red when I was picked last for team sports. I spent years feeling ashamed of my body.

That shame was a waste — a complete and utter waste. It didn't solve anything. It didn't make me better at anything. You cannot criticize yourself into becoming a healthier and happier person.

If you're still in school, I'm probably old enough to be your grandfather. So I hope you'll take some advice from a guy who's been on this planet a lot longer than you have:

There are things that truly matter in life. The shape of your body isn't one of them. What matters are the people you love, the friends you make, the things you learn, and the talents you discover and nurture. And trust me, you probably won't discover your true talents until you're older. My wife (who illustrated this book) began studying art in her late 20s. I didn't try standup comedy until I was 30 — and then I performed in comedy clubs for the next 10 years. I didn't become a software programmer until I was nearly 40. I was almost 50 when I wrote and produced my first film, *Fat Head*.

When you discover your talents, they'll lead you to the most exciting and life-changing missions for The Nautilus. But you can only be the pilot of your own ship, so don't waste your time and mental energy comparing yourself to people who were born to look awesome. Don't waste your life wishing you had their version of The Nautilus instead of yours. Don't waste years thinking that if you exercise enough or starve yourself enough, you'll have a perfect body — and THEN you'll be happy.

It's perfectly good to be good instead of perfect. So focus on being healthy, and then get on with what truly matters in life. That will make you happy.

I didn't write this book to teach you how to look like a model or a professional athlete. I wrote this book because I know life can be a long and wonderful journey. But to enjoy it fully, you need to make that journey in a good ship. Not a perfect ship, not the sleekest or strongest or most beautiful ship, but a good ship.

A good ship is a healthy ship. So take good care of The Nautilus, my young friend, and The Nautilus will take good care of you.

Enjoy the ride.

www.FatHead-Movie.com

Tom Naughton began his professional life as a writer and editor for *Family Safety & Health* magazine. In the many years since, he's worked as a freelance writer, a touring standup comedian and a software programmer. *Fat Head*, his humorous documentary about the lousy health advice handed down from official sources, has been seen on Netflix, Hulu and Amazon Prime, as well as on television networks in several countries. His speeches and other health-related videos have been viewed by millions of people online.

Tom now lives on a small hobby farm in Tennessee with one wife, two daughters, two dogs, one cat, and dozens of chickens.

Chareva Naughton began her art career illustrating forestry training manuals while a Peace Corps Volunteer in Mali, West Africa. She later studied computer animation and web design in Santa Monica, California. Her graphics are included in many of Tom's projects, including his speeches, blog and documentary films. When not hunched over a computer or drawing pad, Chareva enjoys spending time with her family, learning tai chi, gardening and tending to the animals.

....

Please visit www.FatHead-Movie.com/KidsBookSources.html to find the sources used in researching this book.

CPSIA information can be obtained
at www.ICGtesting.com
Printed in the USA
BVHW050950261218
536333BV00026B/3080

9 780998 673400